D1349866

creative

strategic

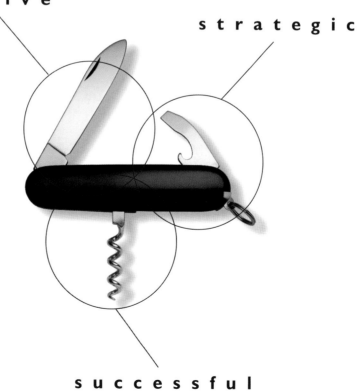

successful

Dedicated to my wife, Susan,
and my sons, Patrick and Andrew,
who still can't believe anyone would pay
me to do what I do.

WHAT'S A SAATCHI
AND HOW COME WE HAVE TWO OF THEM?

How small and mid-sized independent advertising agencies can develop the right tools for survival.

Forward

by Joanne Bischmann, Vice President/Marketing
Harley-Davidson Motor Company

1903 seemed like just another year in most parts of the United States. In the big cities of New York and Chicago, businesses flourished and people strolled streets worn well by horse and carriages. Smaller cities were beginning to rise thanks to factories producing textiles, furniture and machinery.

But 1903 was not just any ordinary year. It was the year that marked the birth of transportation as we know it today. In fact, it defined transportation for the next 100 years. The airplane, the automobile and the motorcycle all made their debut appearances in 1903. You would have expected this advanced, creative and ingenious thinking to have come from one of those booming cities that was the hub of invention and creativity. New York, Chicago or Boston perhaps. But it didn't happen that way. These vehicles with their inventiveness and creative application came from Kitty Hawk, South Carolina; Dearborn, Michigan; and Milwaukee, Wisconsin. Three unexpected cities providing unexpected successes.

I know a little about the birth of that motorcycle in Milwaukee. For more than 10 years, I've been proud to be part of the team that protects and perpetuates the Harley-Davidson brand. Our heritage and the passion, determination and skills of our four founding fathers resonates in everything we do today. The dream that began with three Davidson brothers, Arthur, William and Walter, and their friend William Harley is a dream we seek to fulfill in individuals around the world. Harley-Davidson produced one motorcycle in 1903. Today we sell over 200,000 in more than 47 countries. We ride and interact with over 600,000 members of the Harley Owners Group (H.O.G.), our company sponsored club. We're about to celebrate our 100th Anniversary in which we will honor all those who came before us and their dedication to keeping this brand alive with its integrity intact. We never forget our history but we also don't live in the past. Tomorrow's success will not come from yesterday's sales. We are conscious that we cannot become complacent and we know that there are new ideas and more inventiveness ahead. We take inspiration from our founding fathers who continually reached for new and creative ways to succeed.

Harley-Davidson was recently inducted into the Marketing Hall of Fame as a classic brand. All of us associated with that honor are humbled by it. As keepers of the flame we are deeply aware of the responsibility we hold but also the opportunities it possesses. It requires a sense of protectiveness for the brand, yet a spirit of risk taking is also needed to insure our growth. It takes innovative, creative and strategic marketing.

I didn't learn this at Harley-Davidson. While I have learned a lot about motorcycling and directing marketing activities there, I learned the most crucial advertising and marketing lessons at Hoffman York. Of course, they were called Hoffman York & Compton then. I began my Marketing career as an Account Manager at HY&C in 1985. I can still remember being told that my job was to do anything that was asked, even clean the offices if necessary. (You have no idea how fast we could clean up a mess when a client happened to show up unexpectedly.) I was also told to keep my mouth closed and listen and I would be amazed at what I learned. That was my first lesson and boy, was it a good one. I still give that advice today.

When I left Hoffman York to become Advertising Manager at Harley-Davidson, I remember saying that Harley was getting part of Hoffman York whether they knew it or not. I was just as much a product of that agency as any of their strategic advertising campaigns. They taught me what true creativity could do for a brand and sales. Not to mention, how to negotiate great media plans. They taught me how important marketing is to a company's success.

So besides Hoffman York giving birth to my career, what's the connection to motorcycles? It's simple. Unexpected creativity and life-changing inventiveness do not need to come from big cities. Just like the birth of transportation, great advertising does not have to come from New York, Chicago or Los Angeles. It comes from great minds who are dedicated to success and creativity. It comes from people who are committed to experimenting and challenging the status quo. It comes from people who seek to work with the best. It comes from people who see the joy in their work and more importantly, provide joy to the ones they work for. It comes from excellence in what they do.

Tom Jordan believes all those things. More importantly, he practices them. I know I learned a lot from him. He is a great teacher, although he would never see himself as that. You learn from the multitude of his experiences and maybe more from his passion for this business.

Hoffman York is an unexpected, award-winning advertising agency out of the Midwest. If the leader in motorcycles can come from Milwaukee, perhaps so can a leader in marketing. ❧

AS BROUGHT TOGETHER by the Sigmagraph System 6000 Mark II at ⊕ FOR COLOR INC. Color separations for offset & gravure. 400 S. 5th St., Milwaukee, Wi. 53204. 414-237-4992. Toll Free 1-800-877-7023.

Chapter 1

We weren't always a small, independent agency. Shortly before my arrival, Compton Communications in New York bought Hoffman York. Not too long after that acquisition, Saatchi & Saatchi, London bought Compton.

WHAT'S A SAATCHI
and how come we have two of them?

So Hoffman York & Compton became one of the outposts of the British Empire. We were rubbing shoulders with bigwigs in New York and London. But if we were part of their vast British Empire, we were really more like the small, dedicated band of isolated British soldiers in the movie "Zulu."

As small as we were, they promised us that we were equal partners. And that meant access to all their research data, media clout and, most importantly, a more than equal gathering of our income.

It would have been easy enough to just stay shut up in Milwaukee, but we wouldn't be content with that. We insisted we be given the full respect of the Saatchi empire. When we'd go to London, we'd call on the Saatchi offices. When in New York, Milt Gossitt, President of Saatchi U.S.A., and the whole crew would be our hosts. They put up with us the way the Delta fraternity put up with Flounder in "Animal House." They weren't crazy about us but they didn't exactly know what else to do.

The reason was simple: Even though we were small, we were a source of income. And they were smart enough to realize that including us in their planning sessions and affiliate meetings was a small price to pay for continuing that small, but steady, stream of money.

Unfortunately, after we met the obligatory percentage they sought, we had nothing left for us. And that took its toll.

We all had sore fingers from our new business calls. That's because we only had dial phones. Those new-fangled push button ones were expensive. Believe it or not, even an electric typewriter was a rare perk, coffee was 15 cents a cup (and bad) and we had our own typesetting machine that took up a whole office and looked like one of the crazy contraptions Willy Wonka used to make chocolate. We used to brag to prospects that we had a fully computerized office. We did. One office had one computer.

But what the Saatchis did provide…free of charge…were stories. Leave it to the British to embellish folklore. Any wild ad tale was regaled at the coffee machine (if you had three nickels) as if we shared in their daring. We'd try to impress prospects with the harrowing tales…

"…and they marched into the conference room with telephone books wrapped in brown paper and said, 'We could bore you with all the research. It would take a few hours but we could do that, if you insist.' The client waved it aside and bought the creative ON THE SPOT…."

**If He Were Big Enough
To Fight Back, You Might Think
Twice About Hitting Him.**

Your child can't defend himself against your anger. So for his sake,
call us if you feel your temper getting out of control.
            We'll listen. We'll understand. We'll help. And we'll do our best to
cut your anger down to size.

Parents
Anonymous
963-0566

Copy & Art Direction/Hoffman York & Compton Photography/David VanderVeen Engraving/National Colorite Corp. Printing/HM Graphics

Early '80s.

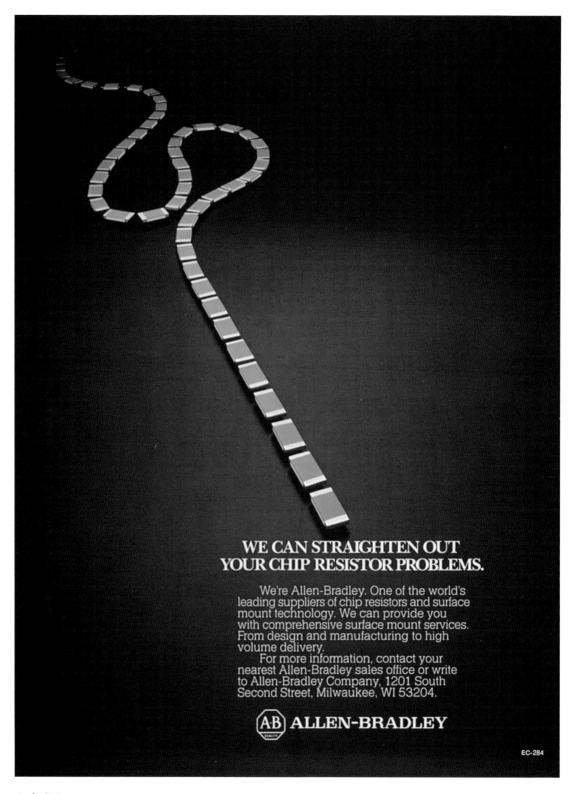

WE CAN STRAIGHTEN OUT YOUR CHIP RESISTOR PROBLEMS.

We're Allen-Bradley. One of the world's leading suppliers of chip resistors and surface mount technology. We can provide you with comprehensive surface mount services. From design and manufacturing to high volume delivery.

For more information, contact your nearest Allen-Bradley sales office or write to Allen-Bradley Company, 1201 South Second Street, Milwaukee, WI 53204.

A·B ALLEN-BRADLEY

EC-284

Early '80s.

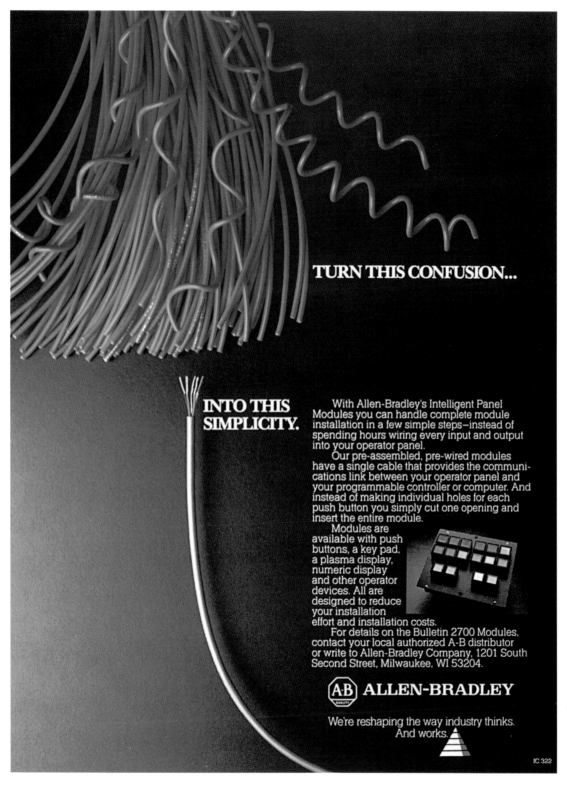

TURN THIS CONFUSION...

INTO THIS SIMPLICITY.

With Allen-Bradley's Intelligent Panel Modules you can handle complete module installation in a few simple steps—instead of spending hours wiring every input and output into your operator panel.

Our pre-assembled, pre-wired modules have a single cable that provides the communications link between your operator panel and your programmable controller or computer. And instead of making individual holes for each push button you simply cut one opening and insert the entire module.

Modules are available with push buttons, a key pad, a plasma display, numeric display and other operator devices. All are designed to reduce your installation effort and installation costs.

For details on the Bulletin 2700 Modules, contact your local authorized A-B distributor or write to Allen-Bradley Company, 1201 South Second Street, Milwaukee, WI 53204.

ALLEN-BRADLEY

We're reshaping the way industry thinks. And works.

IC 322

Early '80s.

"… so the receptionist is filing her nails and ignoring the group of men who were invited to the agency and just when they're ready to leave in a huff a door bursts open and out pop the Saatchis and they tell the prospects that THIS WAS THE PRESENTATION BECAUSE THAT IS HOW THEY TREAT THEIR CUSTOMERS AND UNTIL THAT IS FIXED ALL THE ADVERTISING IN THE WORLD. . . ."

". . .and Maurice Saatchi couldn't stand clients. Once it appeared he would meet one in the hallway by accident and he quickly stopped, pulled out his silk handkerchief and started polishing a door knob . . . ."

The stories were starting to sound like the late night campfire legends of hooks hanging from car doors or the operator shouting, "He's on the other line, get out of the house." Somehow, somewhere they sounded like other stories you heard before.

So even though the Saatchi legends were entertaining, at least to us—not one client ever even chuckled at those stories; they said they sounded like a bunch of snobs—we were going broke trying to pay them.

Taking our inspiration from their own brash acquisition adventures, we decided to make an end run and see if we could buy ourselves back. To our delight we discovered they'd love to remove that little push pin on their worldwide map that was stuck in the midwest of America. (They always confused us with Minneapolis anyway. Something we never felt compelled to correct.) So, after much negotiating in which we pretended that we were really, really, really dumb, they agreed. A rather large group of us went out on a limb, secured loans and began the slow task of working our way out of debt.

We were the first American agency to buy itself back from the Saatchis.

Shortly after we declared our independence from the British Empire, we received calls from most of their other affiliate agencies. Rather than calls of "traitor," they each wanted to know one thing: "How'd you do it? We're thinking of doing the same thing."

We won our freedom … but with our independence from the Saatchis we lost a lot of the resources necessary to satisfy regional and national clients.

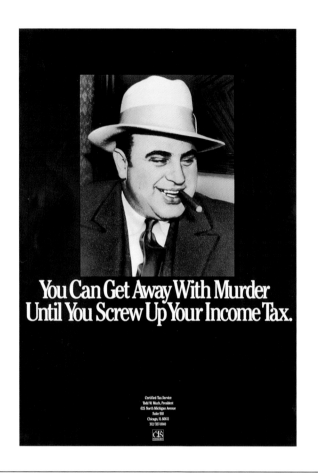

Mid '80s.

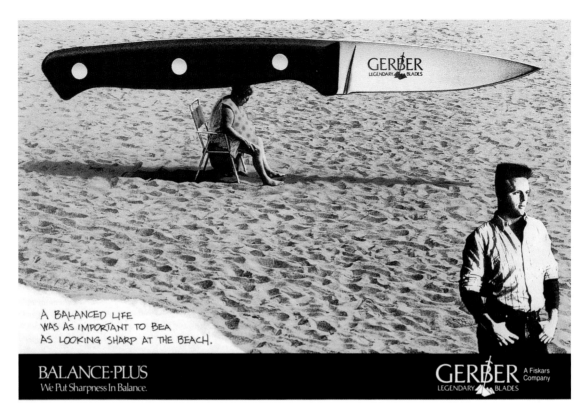

Mid '80s.

If you're in a position like this, you have to find other resources.

The most obvious, but sometimes overlooked place to begin, is the 4As, the American Association of Advertising Agencies. Don't be put off by the fact that all the big agencies are members. Over 60 percent of the agencies in this organization bill less than $10 million per year. This offers a nice range of thinking.

And don't be shy about seeking and using their services. They offer forums on every conceivable topic from leadership training to media relations. They provide a wealth of data for a new business that's just a phone call away. And they are eager to help, regardless of your size.

In addition to the 4As, there are other organizations comprised of small- and mid-sized agencies that have banded together to bring you clout and resources you couldn't provide on your own.

We believe we joined one of the best: AMIN, the Advertising and Marketing International Network (aminworldwide.com). This is a collection of small- and mid-sized agencies all over the world. In the United States it includes the likes of DGWB in Southern California, Turkel Schwartz in Miami, Doe-Anderson in Louisville, Hoffman/Lewis in San Francisco and Bailey Lauerman in Lincoln, Nebraska. From the UK to Japan, India to Australia, this is a fraternity that meets regularly and communicates always. Together we offer more than $2 billion in media spending.

AMIN operates like a fraternity. You can have an open and frank discussion with any member knowing they are forbidden to pitch your business or hire your people. You can talk to a fellow CEO about agency matters that you might not even discuss with your own CFO. All is in confidence, and the learning and sharing is phenomenal.

Each department head meets annually with his/her peers. There is a media conference, a creative conference, a planning conference, an ISO conference, and a CFO conference. You are able to spend three days with people of like mind facing the same problems you do and openly sharing their secrets. It's an invaluable tool. At the Planner's Conference, we had Pam Scott from "Eating the Big Fish" give a special presentation. At the Creative Director's Conference we had Black Rocket offer a seminar on "Selling Scary Creative."

Early '80s.

Ask About
Our Boat Loans.

Early '80s.

TIRED OF UNWANTED FACIAL HAIR?

Your customers are. That's why when it comes to everyday grooming of their large farm animals, they've come to rely on Oster.

The Oster Golden A5 clippers are ideal for general body clipping and frequent touch-up work. Each has a powerful motor for smoother clipping and easier trimming, along with a detachable blade feature for a wide variety of uses.

And only Oster offers a choice: the standard A5 model, and the new Two-Speed A5, with ⅓ more speed on "HI" for the bigger jobs.

So for regular grooming, stock the Oster Golden A5 clippers. Face it, nothing moves like them. And nothing moves off the shelf like them, either.

For more information write Oster Professional Products, Dept. RK, 5055 North Lydell Avenue, Milwaukee, WI 53217.

Oster
Division of Sunbeam Corporation

® Oster © Oster 1988 PET-87-7

Early '80s.

The Senior Management Conferences have been held in France, Italy and England and allow us to tap into global capability.

If you have aspirations to grow, find one of these networks. Investigate which one is right for you and join. The fees will almost certainly be paid back in shared resources. You will benefit greatly from having a network that allows you to conduct online research, shares media clout, and offers an unselfish, sympathetic helping hand whenever you ask.

As one of my AMIN friends has said, "Here is where you'll find your best friends in the business." ❧

Meetings from the Advertising Marketing International Network

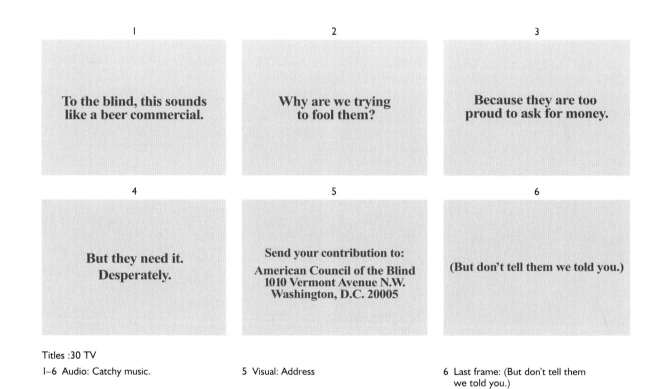

1

To the blind, this sounds like a beer commercial.

2

Why are we trying to fool them?

3

Because they are too proud to ask for money.

4

But they need it. Desperately.

5

Send your contribution to:

American Council of the Blind
1010 Vermont Avenue N.W.
Washington, D.C. 20005

6

(But don't tell them we told you.)

Titles :30 TV

1–6 Audio: Catchy music.

5 Visual: Address

6 Last frame: (But don't tell them we told you.)

Clio-winning TV spot that cost $400.

Chapter 2

Several years ago Keith Reinhard, the head of DDB

Needham, was on stage presenting the winning statues

at the Clio presentation in New York. Before each group

would come up to get their statue, Keith would say

something nice about the winning commercial. National

You've done so much for so long with so little...
you are capable of doing anything with nothing.

campaigns were awarded. Some of the best creative

people in the world climbed up on stage time and time

again to receive their Clios. Keith would offer hearty

congratulations to these big-time players.

But then it came to a category that made Keith stop in his tracks: "Television production under $5,000."

Before he announced the winner, he kept shaking his head and wondering aloud to the audience, "How in the world can anyone produce a television commercial for under $5,000?"

Yes, it was ours. Yes, we won. And no, it wasn't a fluke. In fact, it was so far under $5,000 that my ticket to the Clios and the tuxedo I rented cost more than the commercial we produced. (And if you saw the cheap tuxedo I was wearing, you'd really appreciate how inexpensive our TV spot was.)

In the past eight years, we have produced over a dozen TV commercials that have won at Cannes, the Clios and New York Art Directors Club. They have been featured on television specials in Germany, England, Japan, the United States and Norway.

And each of them cost less than $1,000. Several were only two or three hundred dollars. And most of our "big budget" productions cost a fraction of what other agencies might pay.

Did we do it just to save money for our clients? No. But you might say that was a wonderful side effect.

There are two factors that drive production costs through the roof: 1) agencies create expensive commercials, and 2) production companies demand top dollar.

When I worked at one of the biggest agencies in the Midwest, the production budgets were all well over $100,000. Some packages were up to $500,000. And there is no question about it, the film was gorgeous. But when agencies don't have unlimited resources, they create all kinds of problems for themselves and their clients. The biggest mistake made is not creating an idea within a budget. Too often agencies try to pull off big production ideas on little budgets and the result is a poorly produced commercial that really doesn't do anyone any good.

Some of the secrets we've learned over the years can save everyone a lot of headaches.

First of all, find out what the client can expect to pay. There's a big difference in what you can do for $80,000 versus $30,000.

Secondly, think in simple, minimal terms. Idea generation should be focused on

With an emotional commitment, photography is much more negotiable.

Nancy Reagan :30 TV

1 VO: No matter who you are, when you just can t cut it . . .
2 VO: . . . get a pair of Fiskars scissors.

3 VO: The ones with the orange handle.
4 Visual: First Lady Nancy Reagan unsuccessfully tries to cut ribbon at a ceremony.

5 Logo: Fiskars.

Cannes Silver Lion, $1,000.

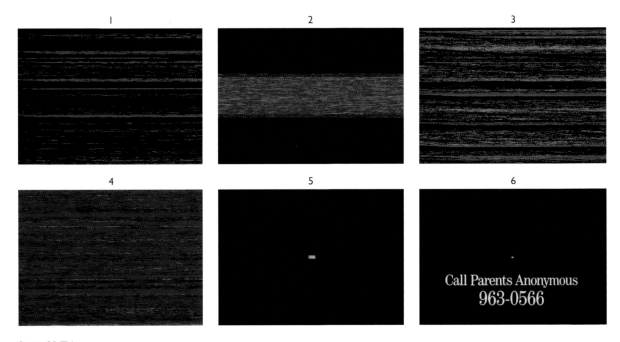

Static :30 TV

1 Audio: Baby crying.
  Visual: Static.
2 Audio: Baby crying louder.

3 Audio: Baby continues to cry louder.
  Woman: Will you stop crying!!!
  Visual: Static turns red as woman s voice gets angrier.
4 Audio: Baby cries louder.
  Woman: Stop crying or I m gonna . . .

5 Visual: Screen goes to black.
6 Visual: Call Parents Anonymous.

Cannes Silver Lion, $500.

See what the new money drives in Beverly Hills.

Come see twenty of the most recognizable autos ever to appear on the silver screen. Jethro's ride in *The Beverly Hillbillies*. The Batmobiles. The Flintstone Mobile. Even the '55 Chevy Harrison Ford drove in *American Graffiti*. And so much more. Now through September 24th. Just one more reason your car belongs at the Petersen Automotive Museum. Call us at 323/930-CARS or visit www.petersen.org.

WILSHIRE @ FAIRFAX

Petersen

AUTOMOTIVE MUSEUM

Hollywood Star Cars
Great Cars of the Movies

Yo! so you thought all sit-down vehicles were for **your old man back home in his Lay-Z-Boy** until you hit those first waves and your **single-chine deep V-hull** breaks right on through leading to that **major cavitation** where your heart may skip a beat but your WaveRunner VXR doesn't **'cuz it's stoked** by Yamaha's 633cc 50 hp marine power plant **which means for heart-rending mind-bending action** your VXR doesn't take a back seat to anyone **brothers and sisters, Amen.**

YAMAHA
Fun that won't quit.

Call 1-800-526-6650 for the Yamaha Water Vehicle Dealer near you.

Flying Colors :30 TV

1 VO: How fast and portable are Wagner's new cordless power painting systems? Just watch.

2 VO: The new cordless power roller automatically pumps paint to cover quickly and easily...

3 VO: ...with no runs or drips.

4 VO: The new cordless power brush is perfect for trimming any job, big or small.

5 VO: Cordless power painting from Wagner. Not just a whole lot faster, a whole lot better.

6 Logo: Wagner.

TV produced for one-half the price of three other bids.

An inexpensive photo... an unbelievable execution.

a strong idea that can stand on its own. Eliminate locations. Eliminate people.

Thirdly, when an idea is formed, find a production company that will offer an emotional commitment to the project. This is key. I've been involved with some big name directors who hold court at lunch, and bully you into doing things their way. But the moment things start to fall apart, their producers are holding court at lunch and the director is taking meetings for the next job.

An emotional commitment can be achieved in a number of ways. If the idea is fantastic, any good emerging director will want it … even at a reduced price … to help build his or her reel. Some directors are pigeon-holed, i.e., only tabletop, only comedy, only cars. They may want an opportunity to show what else they can do. And many of them will take the project … even at a reduced price. Also, a lot of still photographers yearn to get into TV production. The only way they can build a reel is if someone like you lets them … even at a reduced price.

The reason I emphasize "a reduced price" is that when a production company is giving up some of their profit, they can't afford to take your job lightly. They will work their butts off to make it work. They have to.

This approach doesn't rely only on young emerging directors. Some of the proven pros we've worked with will play ball if they like the idea enough. They all become bored to death with "Two ladies in the kitchen," or "Cars shot from helicopter around winding road." These people are creative spirits who want to have fun. Show them a storyboard that's fun and the price tag becomes more negotiable. And the commitment becomes firm.

This same idea applies to still photographers, illustrators and others.

Now I know a lot of the bigger agencies are probably snickering at this suggestion. After all, some of them still make full markup on all production. They'd be giving up big profits. But demonstrate to the world that your passion is in the finished product—not the money—and clients and prospects will respond to you.

* * *

It's important to emphasize that people get excited about great, original ideas. The emphasis should be not just on great … but original.

Around our agency there are three words that can cause instant depression. No, they are not "You are fired," "Cancel the shoot," "Hold all production" or even "Client killed it."

The three words that send defense shields up and can instantly wound even the toughest of egos are simply: "It's been done."

Our agency prides itself on original thinking. Sometimes we carry that to extremes. There have been raging debates in the hallways over the originality of ideas.

"I've seen it before."

"No way."

"Yup. Check the New York Art Directors Annual from 1992."

"What? Where? That was a print ad for a bicycle. This is a radio spot for health care."

"Same idea."

"I didn't know about that when I created it."

"Well, you know it now."

That zest for originality has to be tempered with a client's needs. Clients deserve the hardest working ideas. For the most part those are original ideas. But if something was created for your client and someone points out it was first displayed in a Swedish Awards Annual, you owe it to your client to overlook your ego and create the ad. Your client is trying to sell something. They really don't care about maintaining your pure, creative soul.

But if you do want to maintain a pure creative soul, don't you dare enter it in creative competition.

If it was a brilliant move that helped your client dramatically increase share, it should be entered in the Effies. They measure advertising effectiveness.

But remember, "It's been done."

* * *

You have to examine the types of creative work that exist to appreciate how damaging those words can be to a true creative champion.

Simple, affordable, straightforward.

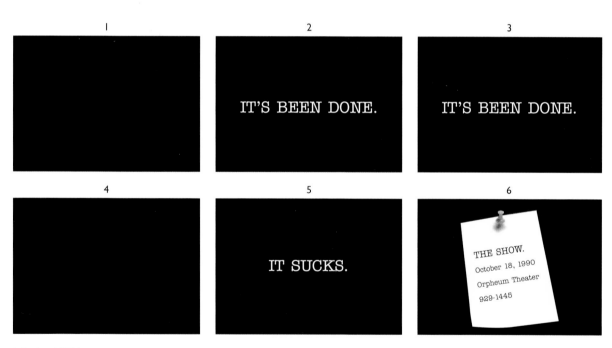

It Sucks. :60 TV

1 Audio: Door opens.
Visual: Blank Screen.
Man 1: Okay, picture this—man walks into a photo booth...
Man 2: Yeah...
Man 1: Yeah, and he's got just little strands of hair that he folds over his head...
Man 2: Um-hm.
Man 1: He's fat... and he tries to get his picture taken, but it keeps flashing at the wrong time, and he even...
Man 2: ...falls down.

2 Man 1: Yeah.
Visual: It's been done.
Man 2: Hamlet Cigars—1988.

3 Man 1: Well, picture this—different guy—stands up— looks you right in the eye and says outrageous things, and you think he's telling the truth, but actually he...
Man 2: He's lying.
Man 1 (weakly): Yeah.
Visual: It's been done.
Man 2: *Saturday Night Live*, 1986 ... and then some car company.

4 Man 1: Okay, I've been saving this one. Two ladies baking a cake, and the one lady is worried because her husband is bringing the boss home for dinner ...
Man 2: Um, the big boss?
Man 1: You got it! But here's the kicker—to prove how moist this cake is, she bakes a goldfish right into it—and ... it lives! It's never been done!
Man 2: For good reason.

5 Visual: It sucks.
Man 1: Oh.

6 VO: Come to The Show—the Minneapolis Showcase of Advertising—and see ideas galore, most of which have never been done before ... none of which ... suck.

Available photography can deliver a fresh idea.

Minimal retouching on a stock photo.

There is a clear, distinctive difference between Original Creative, Adaptive Creative and Borrowed Creative.

Original Creative finds unique ways to deliver a message. Adaptive Creative adapts a technique or idea from someone or somewhere else outside the world of advertising. Borrowed Creative copies advertising techniques that have been created previously.

(There is also Bad Creative that doesn't have an idea, but I won't get into that.)

Original Creative is what deserves the highest praise. Over the years, we've done our fair share of work that can be classified in this regard. It's work that sets a precedent, is truly unique and stands out.

Adaptive Creative uses techniques from television, plays, movies, comedy clubs, books, magazines, etc. and brings it into advertising. There is nothing wrong with this. But for the creative purist (who's like the vegetarian who'll only eat fallen fruit) it's an easy crutch. "Wassssssuppp!" for Budweiser is brilliant advertising. But it wasn't original. It was adapted from a short film. Great. But it had been done.

Borrowed Creative is cheating. Occasionally it happens by accident. Given the same set of circumstances it is possible to come up with a similar conclusion. But too often creative people are looking through the annuals for a technique or idea to rip off. As my good friend Steve Eichenbaum (a true creative champion) often says, "Imitation is the sincerest form of plagiarism."

One of the most ripped-off agencies in modern times (in my opinion) has been Goodby Silverstein. For instance, they created work for Christian Brother's Brandy that used the C B initials. The look was incredible. The idea original. Shortly after, J&B does the same thing. And how about the Norwegian Cruise Line? Marvelously clean. No helicopter shot of the boat. Suddenly everyone and their brother with a cruise line is doing layouts like them.

We've even kept files on agencies that copy other people's ideas. And you'd be amazed how many "creative" agencies are guilty. A few years ago when I was a judge for the National Addys in Washington, D.C., I was discussing this with one of the other judges from a rather prominent agency. In confidence he confessed that most of his ideas were from the awards books. (Note to future panels hiring judges: Make sure they have a good memory and can dismiss the copycats.)

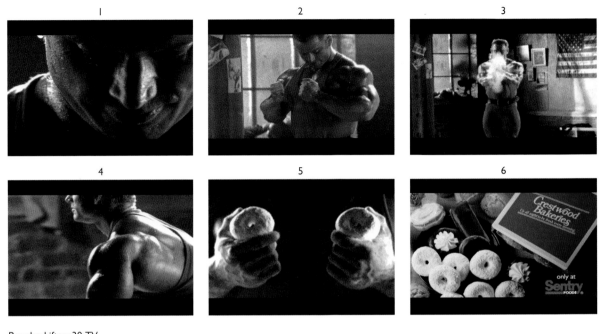

Powder Lifter :30 TV

1 Audio: Music under all.

2 Visual: Weight lifter stretches, flexes arm muscles.

3 Rubs hands with talcum powder.

4 Squats to prepare for lift.

5 Picks up 2 powdered donuts.

6 Logo: Sentry.

Produced for a fraction of actual cost.

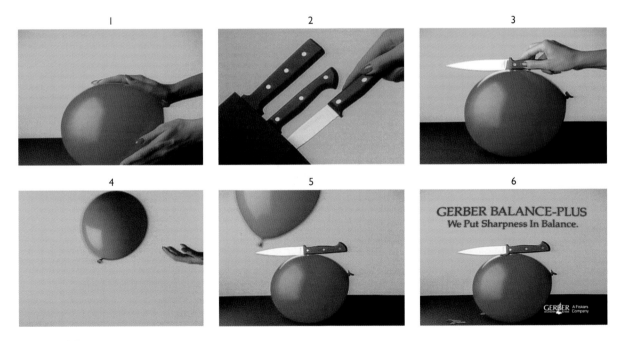

Balloons :30 TV

1 Audio: Music under whole spot.
  Visual: Hand places balloon on table.

2 Visual: Hand selects Gerber knife.

3 Hand balances knife on balloon.

4 Hand tosses second balloon in the air.

5 Balloon hits knife and pops. Knife wobbles, but stays on balloon.

6 Logo: Gerber Balance-Plus.

TV under $10,000.

We created a commercial for *The Show*, the Minneapolis Awards Competition, that used this as the theme. It even won a Silver Award at the New York Art Director's Show. It was met with roaring laughter. I lampooned Joe Isuzu in the spot, a brilliant creation of Della Famina. But this bit was adapted from "The Liar" on *Saturday Night Live*. Ironically, Jerry Della Famina was the keynote speaker at the show. There were quite a few tables filled with folks from his agency. From where I sat, I could just catch the back of his bald head. When the spot aired during the ceremony I swear his head turned so red it seemed to glow in the dark.

When *The Show* book came out, they omitted the entire paragraph in the TV spot "It's Been Done" that made mention of Joe Isuzu. Irony? Perhaps. Extremely adaptive?

Maybe.

And remember, if you want to look at all the wonderful award books, please be careful. Imitate their brilliance to solve tough problems, not how they executed the ad. ❧

Capistrano :30 TV

1 Audio: Howdy folk, I d like to invite you all to the Capistrano Pageant.

2 Audio: Celebrate the first 100 years of California s history. There ll be singers and dancers ...
Visual: Mime starts pantomiming what the cowboy is saying.

3 Audio: ...and even an original play about the old mission. Yep, return to a time when a fella like me can camp under the stars, roam the range ...

4 Visual: Cowboy turns around and shoots the mime.

5 Audio: And even get away with something like that.

6 Audio: C mon, I just winged your jugglin arm. You can still pull a rope, get stuck in a box ...
LOGO: Capistrano Pageant.

Produced for a fraction of real cost.

THERE'S

Throughout much of the world compromise seems to be an accepted way of life. Close is close enough. Perfection is achieved by accident rather than design. Details are unimportant. But on occasion a champion rises to

MORE TO

the forefront and shames those who would settle for less than the best. The wood windows and doors of Weather Shield provide that perfect fit. Look closely at the windows. Let your eyes absorb the beauty of

SEE IN A

True Oak™ interiors. Weather Shield is the only major manufacturer that offers this rich, full grain as an option. Combine that with the gleaming bright-brass hardware, and the beauty it adds to the room is indescribable. Now look even

WEATHER

closer. Sight lines are as clean and smooth as the very glass in the window itself. The joints are screwed, not nailed, to provide a snug, long-lasting fit. And who but Weather Shield has the precision and patience to offer Supersmart? A window

SHIELD

without compromise. Just consider the triple-pane, high-efficiency protection against cold winds and summer suns. Or consider Kleen-Shield™ . . . a window bonded with a special polymer that keeps windows cleaner longer. And they back it

WINDOW.

it all up with a limited 20-year warranty. Cast a cold, calculating eye at Weather Shield. They stand up rather well to any scrutiny. For the name of the Weather Shield dealer nearest you, call 1-800-477-6808 between 8 a.m. and 5 p.m. C.S.T.

WEATHER SHIELD
WINDOWS & DOORS

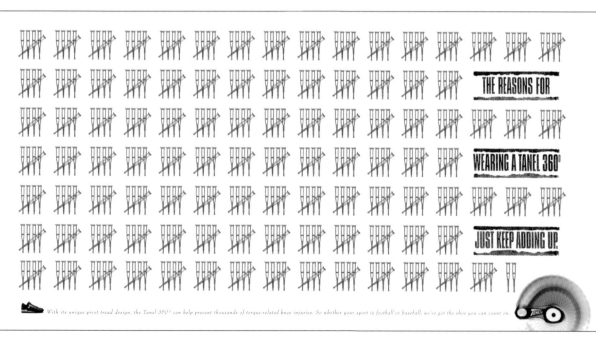

THE REASONS FOR

WEARING A TANEL 360°

JUST KEEP ADDING UP.

With its unique pivot tread design, the Tanel 360° can help prevent thousands of torque-related knee injuries. So whether your sport is football or baseball, we've got the shoe you can count on.

Chapter 3

One advantage you have over all the big shops is that no matter how big they are, they don't own insight or imagination. The power of an idea can belong to anyone, any size. And because of your size you can break down walls inside, and outside, the agency that lead

remember the real business you're in: ideas.

to other opportunities and a better way to work. A few years ago I got a call from Bob Cohen, an old friend who had just taken over the marketing responsibilities at Quaker State. They were between agencies at the time and he needed help. Not with advertising. With ideas.

So several of us would fly to Pittsburgh, rent a car and drive the winding mountains of Pennsylvania to Oil City. The Holiday Inn there was a real treat. It was so cold that winter that ice would form on the inside motel window. Several times I had to take the mattress from the second bed and block the freezing wind blowing under the door.

Small price to pay for the opportunity to work with true marketing pioneers.

Herb Baum was in charge at the time and was bound and determined to continue winning no matter what odds were placed before him.

We were brought in at the tail end of the "4x4 oil positioning." We sat through hours and hours of focus groups. A pattern was emerging. We were discovering that parity could be broken if you came close enough to what we labeled "self-identification." People would tell us "oil is oil" until we asked them to think in a new way. "Would you buy 4x4, an oil specifically designed for harder working engines?" They each owned pick-ups or SUVs. Suddenly oil wasn't oil. They agreed that this new proposition would influence their purchase. Parity was broken. We created advertising that helped reinforce that positioning and it was one of the marketing success stories of the year.

But we weren't through. We listened again to the customers and they kept telling us they wanted the purest, cleanest oil you could buy. For years, the oil industry had been additive crazy. They kept putting chemicals into the oil. We decided to go the other way.

I'm a big believer in talking one-to-one with chemists and R&D. You need to have a working relationship with the people in the labs. We talked directly to their top chemist.

Was it possible to create an even cleaner, clearer oil? Could we filter it one more step?

No problem.

And to demonstrate it, could we put it in a clear bottle?

Water can be hard.

We can be harder.

Gerber presents the first line of faucets designed specifically to combat the damaging effects caused by hard water. With our patented ceramic disk cartridge, we're able to stand up to hard water much better than traditional plastic or metal components.

Recent research indicates that both home owners and contractors understand the effects of hard water and respond instantly to our Hardwater™ Faucets. What does this mean to you? It means you will have, readily available, a product that literally sells itself. But what may prove more amazing is the fact that it's available at a surprisingly competitive price.

And just because we're tough, doesn't mean we're not beautiful. We offer a full range of style and finish options for both kitchen and bath. And back that up with a lifetime warranty against leaks and drips. So get ready with Gerber Hardwater™ Faucets. And get ready for more cold, hard cash.

For more information on the full line of Hardwater™ Faucets, contact your local Gerber Plumbing Fixtures Corporation representative, or call (708) 675-6570.

GERBER
Hardwater Faucets

PROFESSIONALLY MADE. PROFESSIONALLY SOLD. PROFESSIONALLY INSTALLED
© 1995 Gerber Plumbing Fixtures Corp.

The irresistible force, has just met the immovable object.

Gerber presents the first line of faucets designed specifically to combat the damaging effects caused by hard water. With our patented ceramic disc cartridge, we're able to stand up to hard water much better than traditional plastic or metal components.

Recent research indicates that home owners understand the effects of hard water and respond instantly to our Hardwater™ Faucets. What does this mean to you? It means you will have, readily available, a product that literally sells itself. But what may prove even more amazing is the fact that it's also available at a surprisingly competitive price.

And just because we're tough, doesn't mean we're not beautiful. We offer a full range of style and finish options for both kitchen and bath, and the backing of a lifetime warranty* against leaks and drips. So get ready with Gerber Hardwater™ Faucets. And get ready for more cold, hard cash.

For more information on the full line of Hardwater™ Faucets, contact your Gerber Plumbing Fixtures Corporation distributor, or call (708) 675-6570.

GERBER
Hardwater Faucets

PROFESSIONALLY MADE. PROFESSIONALLY SOLD. PROFESSIONALLY INSTALLED
© 1995 Gerber Plumbing Fixtures Corp.
*Contact your Gerber Plumbing Fixtures Corporation distributor for warranty details.

"Hard Water Faucet" positioning that we created.

Problem. But only for the moment. (In addition to open-minded chemists, you need enlightened lawyers. Fortunately, Quaker State had both.)

All came together and Quaker State launched synthetic oil in clear bottles with "Micro Q filtration." Almost overnight it recaptured a disproportionate share of the synthetic oil business. It won Package of the Year honors. But more importantly, without creating an ad, we helped create sales.

That's the power of an idea.

Much the same thinking applied when we repositioned Gerber faucets. They were strictly known as the plumbers' faucets. Sold right off the truck when you called for help. Guys with butt cracks the size of the Grand Canyon were the sales force. (Who said this business isn't glamorous?)

So how could we help? By investigating closer than people had before. We discovered that inside Gerber faucets was a ceramic cartridge. This cartridge made it stronger and wouldn't give way to hairline cracks. And what caused those cracks? Elements in the water.

We decided to reposition them as "The hard water faucets."

Now the plumber could tell a prospect, "Gee, I see what the problem is. You have hard water. I happen to have a hard water faucet in my truck. Want one?"

Boy did they. Sales zoomed.

Again, the power of a big idea.

More and more, we're finding that we have to be flexible for different needs. We offer fully integrated services, as most agencies do, but you have to be prepared to serve a smorgasbord. It might be media only. Creative only. Collateral only. Web only. PR only. But if you find a way to offer perceived value outside the realm of traditional advertising, you'll have an edge over others. And that helps you get in. And it often puts a big name on your roster. That opens eyes. And that helps you get in more doors.

* * *

Another unique angle that agencies our size can provide is with music. It's one of the last creative battlefields. Way too often, some of the bigger shops behave a lot like bigger clients. Too many of them seem to "play it safe." And one of the safest calls has been to hire "jingle houses" for music.

If you've ever worked with some of these places, you know what I mean. So many of them will proudly tell you how they can "get real close to Faith Hill's new song, and still be legal."

Give me a break.

Or, some of the larger clients will insist on buying the rights to a previously produced song because "it instantly offers credibility and familiarity within our target."

Yeah, and it quickly becomes a blur with the thousands of others doing the same thing. You can watch television and hear five songs in a row that are recycled oldies. And we're in a creative business?

So we decided we'd be different. When the right opportunities presented themselves, we started creating our own songs. Not jingles. Songs.

Our first effort was for Children's Hospital of Wisconsin. Despite the fact that they were doing remarkable things, few people could put a face to the name. Our research indicated that people would like them more if they knew them more.

We carved out a positioning: At Children's Hospital of Wisconsin, the child comes first. Within the development of the communications came the opportunity to incorporate original music. So we developed a song, "Who Comes First?" We created the lyrics and melody in house. Then we approached Michael Young in New York. He has produced for Tracy Chapman, Bon Jovi, etc., and we hired him to help us. He lined up an incredible array of musicians, including the lead guitarist from The Band and the back-up vocalist for Aerosmith.

We traveled with our client to New York and magic was made. We cut the song into two-minute and one-minute radio spots. The TV provided the sound track for 60- and 30-second executions. Within days of playing on the radio and TV,

Who comes first :30 TV

1 Lyrics: Who in this world do you love,

2 ...more than you love yourself?

3 Who is worth any sacrifice, if the need is there you wouldn't think twice. Cause ...

4 Who comes first?

5 Who comes first?

6 Visual: The child comes first. Children's Hospital logo.

1

2

3

4

5

6

Ray Charles — Lottery :30 TV

1 Lyrics: You don't have to play to win. You don't have to play to win.

2 It's a natural fact, you get so much back. You don't have to play to win.

3 Anncr: Every year your Wisconsin Lottery has returned over 130 million dollars to property tax relief.

4 This money helps pay your teachers, police and firemen, helps operate parks, libraries, schools and civic centers.

5 Since 1988 your Wisconsin Lottery has returned over 1.5 billion dollars to property taxes. That's a chunk of change.

6 Lyrics: It's a natural fact, you get so much back. You don't have to play to win, yeah. You don't have to play to win.

the stations were flooded with requests for the full song to be played.

Why? It was not only good. It was original...You know, creative?

Since then we have created nearly a dozen different songs for a variety of clients, including writing a song for the Wisconsin Lottery, performed by Ray Charles that Victor Vanacore scored.

Some people may tell you they don't have the talent on staff to do it. Tell them to go outside. Search the coffee house and blues bars. They're out there. You're smaller, you're flexible. You can find a way.

* * *

Keep in mind that your size can be an advantage. If you're not arrogant and can keep an open mind, you can tap into the creative potential that exists throughout the entire agency.

At some of the bigger agencies, a creative person could spend their whole career and never get to know the media department. The media folks are often kept on different floors, so unless you introduce yourself on an elevator, they are easily mistaken for the accountants. During meetings, a whispered command will tell media they have to present last in case time runs short. And no matter how much they have to say...cut it in half.

For a few of the big shops media is the proving ground for all the "account guy wannabes." Yet the account people treat the media folks the way physicians treat chiropractors.

At our agency we've learned that the best way for a mid-sized agency to operate is to give media the respect and support they deserve. Because when you include media early on you'll not only save yourself a lot of aggravation later, you can develop unique creative.

A quick look at the operation of a traditional agency has the account group coordinating all the action. And that's fine. But sometimes they get just a little too close to being the client. Balance, all the way around, is key.

The account planner brings to the assignment the motivation of the consumer.

He or she serves as the alter ego of that audience.

With the account group "what" to do is decided. If the media department or the media and account group decide "how" to do it without key creative collaboration, you're putting unnecessary handcuffs on the creatives.

If you want to see your budgets eaten up in a hurry with fractional page ads and spot radio that "deliver the reach and frequency within the budget parameters," exclude your media folks from the creative planning.

The best way to get media, account service and creative all on the same wavelength is to provide a common wavelength. For advertising, we believe the one and only true measure is Net Takeaway. What does the consumer get out of the message?

I'm a big believer in analogies. To me, advertising is like golf. Your planner provides the club selection. The marketing from your account people is like the driver for distance to the fairway. The creatives have the wedges and putters once you're in reach.

But let's face it, the goal of golf isn't to see how many clubs you can use. It's how few strokes it takes to get the ball in the hole.

Work with media and you've got a good caddie. But you have to ask them questions. "Do you think I can cut this dogleg over the trees and stay out of trouble? Can we use fractional page island ads instead of just one spread and dominate the publication? The wind is blowing right in our face and there's a 20 degree elevation; three wood to the green or go for a better approach . . . has anyone ever used outdoor timed with radio during rush hour so they can see and hear our message at the same time?"

And surprise, surprise, beneath every good media person isn't an account wannabe, it's a living, breathing creative champion. Put them in the conceiving stage and you'll be amazed at the far-out solutions they recommend. It's as if someone took the governor off the go-cart. They want to go full speed. Creative people are telling them, "Oh, that may be a little too wild." It's a great way to spark the process. And a great way to tap into the creative brains that exist outside copywriters and art directors.

It also gives you a strong ally against "tried and true, let's not rock the boat, it ain't broken" thinking. They become advocates of "why not?" to help you battle all the "whys?"

I've worked at several big agencies that seemed to have inadvertently departmentalized egos. A creative person with a marketing idea might be ridiculed. A research person with a media proposal was left behind the glass of a focus group. And anyone who had an ad idea who wasn't in the creative department (God forbid...a client) was just stared at with disgust and amazement as if they just coughed up a fur ball.

At our place we struggle (and it honestly is a struggle) to maintain a collective ego. A good idea is a good idea, regardless of who created it. We try to have enough confidence in our individual abilities to not be intimidated by suggestions from anyone.

It's interesting how clients pick up on that. They begin to realize that for the same dollar spent they get more people worrying about every aspect of their business.

No matter what size agency you have, try it. You'll be amazed how everyone will respond...especially the media people. If nothing else, they'll get to see how the people who come to work with ponytails actually do make a contribution to advertising.

But don't be surprised if some of the media folks start wearing all black. ❧

Most of us are hypocrites. I don't mean that as a slam, it's really just an honest observation. We tell our clients that they should stand apart from their competitors, look and feel distinctive and have a

the shoemaker's children.

unique point of view. But 99 percent of us get up in front of a prospect and look and act the same, promise the same things, even dress the same.

Take this little test—Have you ever told a prospect that you:

· *represent breakthrough creative?*

· *treat your client's money as if it's your own?*

· *place media more cost-effectively than anyone else?*

· *pay attention to the details?*

· *act as your client's partner?*

If you answered "yes" to more than one, you are not alone.

And that's the problem.

More than likely you've had long planning sessions on how to position your agency but just couldn't come to a consensus. Some of the ideas were too wacky, too "out there," too risky. And if a few folks got really uncomfortable, well then, you retreated back to saying things you thought the prospect would want to hear. (If a client ever told you that they didn't want to be different, just wanted to be safe, you'd hear doors slamming all over the agency, wastebaskets getting kicked and people swearing a blue streak about the gutless client.)

Let's face it, we can be gutless too.

Positioning yourself with distinction takes more than just intelligence and insight. It takes courage.

For starters, you have to remove yourself from the process. Take your ego out of it. Begin by talking in the third person about your shop. Give it a different name for this exercise. Remove ego and you begin to remove fear.

Now, get your best and brightest people involved. And make sure some of them are brand new to the place. They aren't jaded and they tend to be thrilled to be working at a fabulous place like yours. (*Us? Fabulous?* Yes.)

Agree to disagree and agree that nothing you create will be perfect. Don't dwell on what something *doesn't* do. Work harder on what something *can* or *might* do.

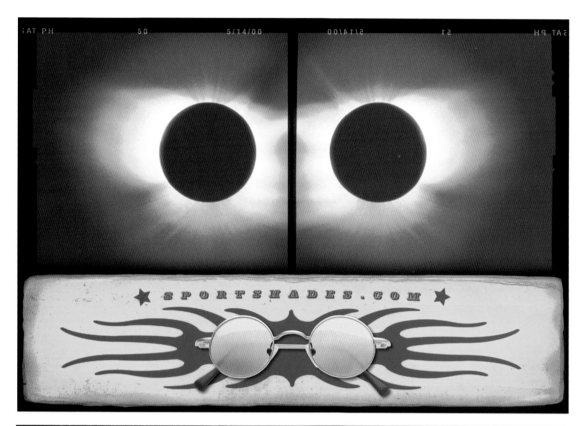

Small clients provide a great creative opportunity to decorate your walls with eye-popping art.

The colors are okay. But we'd prefer the image of a toxic dump. BOY IS THAT AN UGLY SHIRT.™

YOU'LL FEEL JEALOUS THE FORK GETS INTO IT BEFORE YOU DO.

START SPREADING THE NEWS. *Anthony's* N.Y. Style Cheesecakes & Coffee Shop   1660 N. WATER STREET 278-8668

AFTER YEARS OF DEBATE,

WE FINALLY GAVE IN TO

AUTOMATION. YOU'LL

NOW FIND PUSH BUTTON

TELEPHONES IN THE LOBBY.

Schilke

TRUMPETS HANDCRAFTED WITHOUT COMPROMISE.

YOU'VE BEEN LOOKING FOR IDEAS IN ARCHITECTURAL DIGEST.
WHEN ALL ALONG THERE IT WAS, IN DR. SEUSS.

CONTEMPORARY FURNISHINGS IN THE THIRD WARD. OPEN MONDAY THRU FRIDAY 10-8.
SATURDAY 10-5 & SUNDAY 12-5. VISIT US AT 224 E. CHICAGO STREET. OR CALL 278-8100. | **RUBIN'S**

(How many times has a client been less than thrilled when the test scores show that 40 percent of the audience showed an intent to purchase and they worry about the other 60? This is the same thing. If the greatest minds of all advertising in history couldn't solve this perfectly, what makes you think you will?)

Try.

After many positioning exercises like this, we landed on something for us. Is it distinctive? Very much so. Is it memorable? Oh, yes. Is it perfect? Far from it. Does everyone buy into it? Most of us do.

After surfing the web and reading all the long-winded agency philosophies that basically said all the same thing, Managing Partner Troy Peterson had an idea that we could eliminate the bullshit and instead offer a symbol...the multi-utility knife. We had them specially made with three tools: a blade, a can opener and a corkscrew.

The blade represents creative, the can opener represents strategic thinking and the corkscrew represents success. By symbolizing our capabilities this way, we appear different from our competitors. This became our visual invitation to Hoffman York.

You'll find it on our letterhead, our business cards, our web site, our wearables. If someone asks, "Are you those knife people?" we've won. Because no one says, "Are you that collection of names I've heard of that represents breakthrough thinking?"

Great. That's who we are and what we do. But how do we do it differently and better than anyone else?

The next step is to find a way to present your *passages to insight* in a unique and memorable manner. Again, too many agencies show flow charts with circles and diagrams and arrows flowing into boxes. Can you imagine asking a sculptor how she creates her work? *"This square represents the initial thought and that flows into this balloon with a light bulb that indicates the emerging of inspiration. From there, follow this arrow up to this red box with 'step three' written on it. At this stage I select the proper material and test that against the target audience for their acceptance of etc., etc."*

Our hallways serve as a gallery of our work.

Main entrance.

Insight is not always a linear process. Yet we feel compelled to imitate manufacturers and deliver a "just in time" inventory equation for idea generation.

We decided it was better to embrace a heroic thought that allows insight to come from any number of directions. We call it *The Inner Voice.* We believe there is an inner voice in the brand, the consumer, the competition, the package. It whispers. It warns. It tells you something that other voices avoid. It's a beacon to the path you seek. It can be trusted. It's true.

By embracing a heroic thought, heroic efforts can be achieved. Much of the same due diligence as always is applied (focus groups, shadow shopping), but this encourages an open mind to other methods and stimuli.

The Inner Voice allows us to present ourselves in a unique manner that symbolizes an agency relying more on the magic of what we do than on just hard, rational thoughts.

Again, does everyone here unanimously agree that this is how we should portray ourselves? No...but most do.

We didn't just try to appease everyone, because in the past that led us to impressing no one.

Be bold. Have courage. Listen to your inner voice. Be somebody. Be something.

* * *

But today, even that's not enough. Where do you live? I don't mean your house, I mean your office. Is it magical? Does it inspire your people? Does it signal to the world that magic happens there?

In today's world your clients typically have more money than you do. So they can buy better computers than you. So they can install QuarkXPress and fiddle around, and gosh isn't this advertising thing easy? Within many major corporations you have a whole cadre of in-house advertising creative hopefuls.

Typically, they are extremely good at what they do. But they also want a crack at what you do. Because it's more fun. Your physical plant has to send a signal that you are different from your clients.

For that very reason, three years ago, we decided to start from scratch and build a whole new place. But I'll warn you right now, if you build from scratch prepare to itch. A lot.

Granted, even though our old offices weren't impressive, there was something nice about working in a dorm-like atmosphere. A lot of the smaller shops seem to end up that way. You can spill coffee on a conference table, roll bowling balls down the hallway (a beat-up tuba was the target), bounce basketballs off the walls, stick pencils in the ceiling, and shove lit firecrackers under someone's door. But after about, oh, 10 years, it takes its toll. We got used to it. But prospects were less than impressed. It was like meeting someone for the first time and inviting them over for a cup of coffee…to your double-wide trailer filled with cats.

In our business image is so important. And if we wanted to take that next step toward attracting bigger and better clients, we needed to improve that image. The timing was right. We were outgrowing our space (even though it would have been fun to remove a wall or two…physically). And we looked around the city for a larger Class A space. There was only one we found that we all liked. It was at 1000 North Water Street. The 16th floor. Never occupied. A blank canvas.

The owner was intrigued at the prospect of having an advertising agency as a tenant. Everyone else in this high-rise was a lawyer or investment counselor. We were weird. And he liked that.

So we inked the deal, hired a top-flight designer and proceeded to create a brand new house for our agency.

The problem was, the moment we agreed, the blinders we all had been wearing at our old place came off and we hated going to work. I was spotted many times with scissors in hand cutting frayed carpet. One employee whose partner is a hair stylist insisted we could get his friend to do it cheaper than my hourly rate. (Ha, ha.)

The way we were.

The way we are.

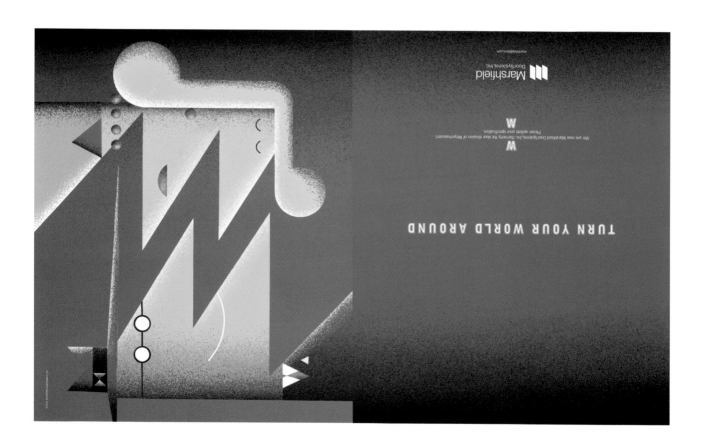

We were good clients. When we'd ask the designer what something would look like he usually said "It'll be cool." That's what we wanted to hear.

Now if you've done any building or remodeling on a house, you know that nothing ever runs smoothly. Or on time. Or on budget. Things drag. Expenses keep creeping higher and higher. And tempers seem to rise everywhere. It's really hard to keep your cool with a carpenter who promises to be there and never shows up. Or someone delivering the wrong desk. Or workers who scratch your new conference room table. (At the old place we would have laughed and joined in by carving our initials on the table.)

The entire process is like being awake during an operation. You really get nervous hearing the doctor say, "Now, where does that thing go again?" Days turned to weeks. Weeks turned to months. And the operation continued. Finally, just when we were at our wit's end, it . . . was . . . finally . . . finished.

Our dream was realized. We had a cool space. So cool that clients started hanging out with us, and sticking around. They really liked it. But we weren't prepared for the reaction from the rest of the tenants.

When the elevator would stop at 16, as our blue-jeaned folks with berets and pierced body parts would get out, the three-piece suits just had to offer their comments. "Do you think they'll ever get carpeting?" "What's up with all those wires and lights?"

It got to the point that they thought every Speedy Messenger worked at our place. "Sixteen, right?" No. One account person had a big meeting and she wore a suit. When she pushed 16, she was practically attacked. "No, honey, you must have the wrong floor."

After a few months when they realized we didn't spread disease or threaten their lifestyles, they gradually warmed up to the weirdos in their midst.

But every once in awhile, just to shake them up, someone will pull out a harmonica and serenade them on the way down.

Yeah, they just love that. ❧

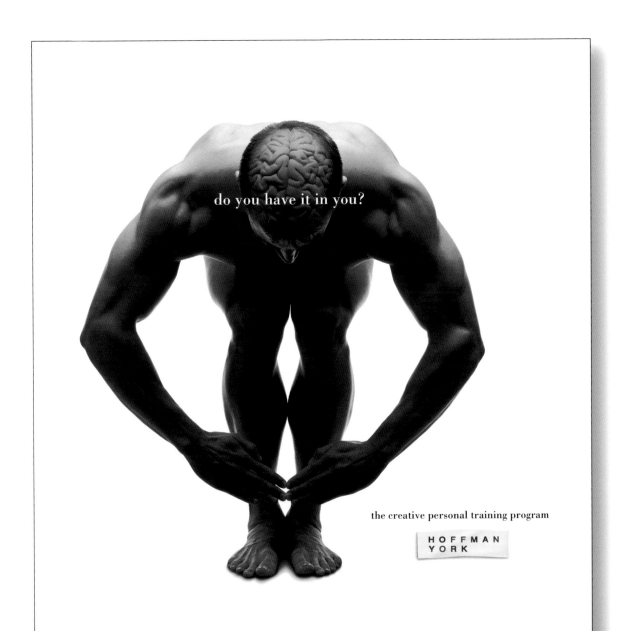

Someone once observed that the inventory of our "factory" goes down the elevator at the end of the day. And according to most industry data, our staff represents about half of all our expenses. So it

the importance
of culture, identity and professional growth.

stands to reason that good people need to be protected, potential stars need to be groomed, and an environment that brings out the best in everyone needs to be fostered. Easier said than done.

My experience helps me a lot in my day-to-day dealings with employees. No, not my experience in advertising, my experience in the Army. I was a prison guard.

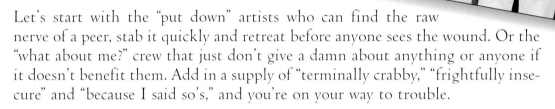

I gave a speech in Toronto last year and the slide that got the most laughs simply said, "Don't hire jerks." For some reason our industry is filled with people who have the ability to screw up harmony every chance they get.

Let's start with the "put down" artists who can find the raw nerve of a peer, stab it quickly and retreat before anyone sees the wound. Or the "what about me?" crew that just don't give a damn about anything or anyone if it doesn't benefit them. Add in a supply of "terminally crabby," "frightfully insecure" and "because I said so's," and you're on your way to trouble.

But my biggest personal gripe is with the "incurable ad nerds." They think they're good because they can rattle off statistics about other creative people who *are* good. A solid majority of these folks can be real jerks. Placate this group and you can be headed for disaster. Why? Because they don't care about commerce. They don't care about what's right. They don't care about anything other than seeing their name in an ad annual. Some of them will sacrifice a client's best interest, put the agency in a bad light and then be gone when you're facing the consequences.

In a large agency, people like this can hide for a long time. But in a smaller place they can be a cancer, disrupting everyone and making good, solid employees believe less in themselves. Before you hire anyone, look for the warning signs: a resume that mocks any of the places they worked; subject matter in their books that you wouldn't show to your mother; constant references to awards that are not balanced by a need to help a client sell their goods or services.

Now I recognize that it's impossible to attract only nice people. And this business requires a certain "edge" for your shop to be progressive and hip. But be careful not to get overloaded with nerds.

"Fine," you say, "but I have trouble attracting even warm bodies. Where do I get these talented people who are nice?"

If you can't find them, grow them.

How?

Remember gym class back in high school? Mostly it was a lot of organized calisthenics that did a pretty good job of general conditioning.

After high school, if you joined a gym, you were on your own. So, rather than do full squats (which hurt like hell) or military presses, you worked more on the bench press and curls. And when you got tired, or didn't feel like working out, you let it slide.

But then someone suggested you try a personal trainer.

A trained, objective eye to determine what you needed and how to get there. No longer could you avoid the exercises you hated. Your trainer made you do them. And no longer could you continue with the exercises you liked so much…they weren't helping where you needed help most. And when you didn't feel like exercising you weren't allowed to quit.

Anyone who has ever had a personal trainer will tell you that the process is somewhat painful, but the results are incredible.

At Hoffman York Fitness we have incorporated this technique to train every person in the agency.

• *First, we select our trainers.*

Look around the agency at every level. Who is a good leader? Who is smart and determined and not shy about standing up to someone who may outrank them? Not a jerk…not someone who would/could use this position unwisely…someone who can politely urge another agency member to strive to become his/her best.

We selected 15 trainers. We made sure that no one was given more than five trainees. And we made sure that the trainer and trainee were not from the same department.

do you have it in you?

personal trainers wanted

HOFFMAN YORK

(i.e., I have a Planner and our Research Director as my trainees. My trainer is an Account Supervisor.)

· *Assign the groups.*

Who is the most compatible? If you have a domineering Type A account person, select a strong, even-tempered media planner as his/her trainer.

Warning: Don't overload your trainers if they are already burning the midnight oil. Give those people fewer trainees.

· *Agree on common objectives.*

Make sure all the trainers understand what is expected of them and their trainees. Have a written description of the desired effect for each and every person. This starts broadly (department expectations).

An example: We wrote a description of what we want each of our creative people to become:

A fun-loving individual who has a fresh and unique perspective on how to capture the heart and mind of the consumer. Someone who understands and enriches strategy, and is prolific in developing insightful and imaginative ideas. Has a discerning eye for what is right for the personality and character of the Brand. Is innately curious, and constantly challenges herself/ himself to do work that advances the Brand, the category, the client and the industry. Mindful of what is achievable. Is able to defend a point-of-view and is adept in creating excitement, enthusiasm and buy-in for the idea. A team player who inspires creativity in others.

A description like the above is written for every department, every level.

Just because we have trainers doesn't mean we gave up on the calisthenics. We have overall seminars for the entire professional staff. Examples: Creative Use of Media, Innovative Ideas in Research. We'll even bring in outside speakers, like we did with Rich Bailey, President of Bailey Lauerman Advertising, who spent a morning sharing his creative philosophy with the staff. That was a big hit.

· *Personal assessment of each trainee.*

Using the department descriptions as a beginning point, we determine opportunities for individual improvement. This is a mutual contract. Everybody is asked where they feel they could improve the most. The trainer uses this, plus input from the trainee's supervisor, to create an individual training program.

For demonstration purposes, using the creative example above, we might agree that a copywriter needed to enhance his/her understanding of strategic importance. Perhaps this person has shown a tendency to ignore input and just starts "executing." Maybe this same person is leaning too much on the award books for inspiration, so the work isn't as fresh as it could be.

In a positive way, we would structure a program that would help this person grow stronger in these areas.

An organized, digestible program is put in place.

For the above creative example, it might begin with a subscription to *Brand Week*. The trainer might assign a reading list that includes *Eating the Big Fish* and other books that champion positioning and branding. Monthly lunch sessions might be arranged to discuss what has been read. Articles from Donny Deutsch and others who belittle the creatives who copy the awards books might be sent to every creative person as an "interesting point of view" (you don't want to rub their noses in it).

This is where it gets fun because you can do anything. Part of my trainee's program includes riding the bus more often and attending tractor pulls. Just to make sure she stays in touch with more than one audience.

· *Agree to be flexible.*

We have busy lives. We have to be prepared to not let this interfere with work or family. But even directionally we've seen results. For myself, I've read more books than I ever would have on my own.

You may find something else works better for you. But we've been more than pleased with the results.

And now our nice people are even smarter. ❧

© 1990 Caballo Buenos Aires

A LAND WHERE FEW ROADS ARE PAVED, AND SPEED IS A NATIONAL PASSION, FOUR WHEEL DRIVE COULD ONLY BE A BEGINNING. BECAUSE SPEED HAD TO BE SACRIFICED TO MAINTAIN EVEN A SEMBLANCE OF CONTROL. BUT TION THAT CAN ROB YOU OF CONTROL.

YOU DON'T STEP INTO A CABALLO XL. YOU PUT IT ON. THE MOMENT YOU EASE BEHIND THE FIFTH WHEEL, YOU BECOME PART OF THIS AUTOMOBILE. AND IT BECOMES PART OF YOU. BECAUSE THE CENTRAL

INTRODUCING THE WORLD'S FIRST FIVE WHEEL DRIVE

LIFE IN THE LAND OF THE GAUCHOS WITHOUT THE EXHILARATION OF EXCEEDING 160 KM/H ON A REGULAR BASIS WAS BECOMING SIMPLY UNACCEPTABLE.

ENTER THE CABALLO XL. AND THE EVOLUTION OF THE FIFTH WHEEL. CONVENTIONAL AUTO TECHNOLOGY HAS THE STEERING WHEEL RIGIDLY ANCHORED TO A GEAR REDUCER. AND THAT GEAR REDUCER HAS ALWAYS BEEN FIRMLY RIVETED TO THE MAIN FRAME. ON A SILKY SMOOTH HIGHWAY THAT MAY BE FINE. ON A ROUGH ROAD IT CAN TRANSLATE TO A TOTAL LOSS OF CONTROL.

AND EVEN WORSE ... A BARRIER TO HIGH SPEED.

THE CABALLO XL HAS CHANGED THAT FOREVER. WE'VE INTRODUCED A UNIQUE SHOCK ABSORBING SYSTEM TO THE ENTIRE STEERING COMMAND, INCLUDING WHEEL, SHAFT AND DRIVER'S SEAT. BY INTEGRATING THE STEERING WHEEL TO THE SEAT WE'VE ISOLATED IT, AND YOU, FROM THE FRAME. THAT, IN TURN, VIRTUALLY ELIMINATES ALL OF THE BONE SHATTERING VIBRA-

COMPUTER ACCEPTS RAW INPUT FROM THE STEERING SENSOR AND ENTERS THE DATA INTO THE ACTIVATION PROGRAMMER BACKUP. THE DATA IS ALSO TRACKED INTO A SCRATCHPAD MEMORY. THIS INFORMATION TRANSLATED CAN ACTUALLY ANTICIPATE AND COMPENSATE FOR THE ROUGH ROAD LONG BEFORE YOU DO.

NOW OTHER AUTO MAKERS MAY BEGIN THEIR MESSAGES BY BOASTING ABOUT ANTI-LOCK BRAKES, A STRAIGHT SIX 228 HP BREATHING THROUGH 24 VALVES, AND NOKIA HAKKAPELIITTA TIRES. WE HAVE ALL OF THAT, TOO. BUT WE FEEL THIS IS WHERE THAT NEWS BELONGS. AT THE THE END OF THE ANNOUNCEMENT OF WHAT WILL CERTAINLY BECOME THE NEXT GENERATION OF AUTOMOBILE.

CABALLO XL.
THE WORLD'S FIRST FIVE-WHEEL-DRIVE SPORTS CAR.

Introductory "April Fool's" ad for the Caballo XL.

Chapter 6

One day we were sitting around feeling sorry for ourselves. (Something creative departments do everywhere on a regular basis.) First we complained about how much work we had to do. (Don't ever have this discussion with a paramedic or a Peace Corps volunteer. They tend to

If the world won't come to you, create a new world.
The world's first five-wheel-drive car.

blink a lot in disbelief.) Then we complained about how tough it was to sell great creative. But then we settled into our usual gripe about not being included in more of the glamorous pieces of new business.

One of the phenomenons of the advertising business is that clients tend to look for agencies that already have related industry experience. It doesn't matter that you did lousy work with that experience. One of the first screening questions they ask is "Well, do you have any _____ experience?"

The usual reply is "No, but we have people on staff with _____ experience when they worked at another agency."

"I'm sorry," they reply. "We're only looking at agencies that currently have _____ experience."

Now, to me this has always been confusing. I can understand the need for exact related experience in, say, medicine. I wouldn't want a gynecologist to perform an appendectomy. But in our business we are, first and foremost, salespeople. And a good salesperson can sell just about anything.

On that particular day we were moaning about the stories in the ad press that the Alfa Romeo account was supposedly coming up for review. And unless we had a well-known national reputation or related imported car experience, there was no way in the world they would consider us. Now or in the future.

That's when the idea struck. Okay, I thought, maybe we don't have a car account, but what if we convinced the world that we did?

The idea wasn't sinking in. Everyone just kind of stared at me.

"No, really," I began. "It's simple. We create a car, develop the marketing position, create the advertising, produce it and even fool the experts."

A unified look of "You must be nuts" filled the room. But I wouldn't give in.

"I know we could do it. It would be a lot of work, but I know we could do it."

It took awhile for everyone to accept the idea. But every time an objection was raised, it became a new creative opportunity.

"They know their own business. How can you fool the auto world?"

"We'll say it's a brand new car."

THERE WAS A TIME WHEN NO CAR IN THE WORLD COULD GLIDE ALONG THE ROUGH, WINDING ROADS OF ARGENTINA WITHOUT PAUSE.

THAT TIME WAS LAST YEAR.

BUT THIS YEAR THERE'S THE CABALLO XL, THE WORLD'S FIRST (AND ONLY) FIVE WHEEL DRIVE AUTOMOBILE. WITH ONE BOLD SWEEP IT WILL REVOLUTIONIZE WHAT YOU ACCEPT IN A SPORTS CAR, AN ALL-TERRAIN VEHICLE … OR BOTH.

BEFORE CABALLO XL, THE LAST VEHICLE TO FLY OVER THIS ROAD WAS 5,000 METERS ABOVE IT.

© 1990 Caballo Buenos Aires

CONVENTIONAL TECHNOLOGY HAS LONG OVERLOOKED THE MOST IMPORTANT WHEEL IN YOUR CAR, THE STEERING WHEEL. BUT UNLIKE ALL THE LEMMINGS IN THE AUTO WORLD, WE NO LONGER FIRMLY ANCHOR THE STEERING COLUMN TO THE MAIN FRAME. INSTEAD, WE'VE INTRODUCED A UNIQUE SHOCK ABSORBING SYSTEM TO THE ENTIRE STEERING COMMAND. WHEEL

SHAFT AND DRIVER'S SEAT ARE INTEGRATED INTO A SMOOTH FLOWING UNIT.

THIS VIRTUALLY ELIMINATES THE VIBRATION THAT DENIES YOU STEERING CONTROL.

ADD TO THAT AN ONBOARD COMPUTER THAT TRANSLATES ROAD INFORMATION SO QUICKLY AND ACCURATELY, IT CAN AUTOMATICALLY COMPENSATE FOR THE IRREGULARITIES OF THE ROAD FASTER THAN YOU CAN.

THE RESULT IS UNSURPASSED CLARITY OF COMMAND.

BUT WHAT GOOD IS CONTROL WITHOUT SPEED AND PERFORMANCE?

WE ANSWER THAT WITH A STRAIGHT SIX 228 HP ENGINE, ANTI-LOCK BRAKES, AND OUR DOUBLE TREAD NOKIA HAKKAPELIITTA TIRES. ALL STANDARD.

SO TEST DRIVE A CABALLO XL ON A ROCKY ROAD NEAR YOU. BUT PLEASE NEVER CLOSE YOUR EYES.

YOU MIGHT THINK YOU'RE FLYING.

CABALLO XL.
THE WORLD'S FIRST FIVE-WHEEL-DRIVE SPORTS CAR

CABALLO XL IS NOT THE FIRST PERFORMANCE CAR TO TRY TO TEMPT YOU WITH A STRAIGHT SIX 228 HP ENGINE OR ANTI-LOCK BRAKES. OR NOKIA HAKKEPELIITTA STEEL BELTED RADIALS.

WE'RE OF THE OPINION THAT HORSEPOWER NEEDS TO BE ENJOYED AT FULL SPEED REGARDLESS OF TERRAIN.

GRATES THE ENTIRE STEERING COMMAND. WHEEL, SHAFT AND DRIVER'S SEAT ARE COMBINED INTO A SMOOTH FLOWING UNIT THAT VIRTUALLY ELIMINATES THE VIBRATION THAT DENIES YOU

© 1990 Caballo Buenos Aires

TODAY, THAT'S JUST THE OPENING ANTE TO THE UNCOMPROMISING AUTO ENTHUSIAST.

YET THOSE OTHER SO CALLED SPORTS CARS LOSE ALL SPORT THE MOMENT THE HIGHWAY GETS A LITTLE ROUGH. BUT THAT'S WHERE OUR FUN BEGINS.

BECAUSE THE CABALLO XL IS THE WORLD'S FIRST (AND ONLY) FIVE WHEEL DRIVE VEHICLE. WE'VE RECOGNIZED THAT THE STEERING WHEEL IS EVERY BIT AS IMPORTANT TO PERFORMANCE OFF ROAD AS ANY WHEEL THAT HITS THE GROUND. SO UNLIKE ALL THE OTHERS WHO INSIST ON ANCHORING THE STEERING COLUMN TO THE MAIN FRAME, WE'VE LIBERATED IT.

THE CABALLO XL HAS A UNIQUE SHOCK ABSORBING SYSTEM THAT INTE-

STEERING CONTROL.

ADD TO THAT AN ONBOARD COMPUTER THAT TRANSLATES ROAD INFORMATION SO QUICKLY AND ACCURATELY IT CAN AUTOMATICALLY COMPENSATE FOR THE IRREGULARITIES OF THE ROAD FASTER THAN YOU CAN.

THE RESULT IS UNSURPASSED CLARITY OF CONTROL.

SO IF YOU'RE THE KIND OF PERSON WHO NOT ONLY SPEEDS UP ON THE CURVES, YOU'RE READY TO IGNORE THEM, YOUR CAR IS READY.

CABALLO XL.
THE WORLD'S FIRST FIVE-WHEEL-DRIVE SPORTS CAR

Follow-up ads for Caballo XL.

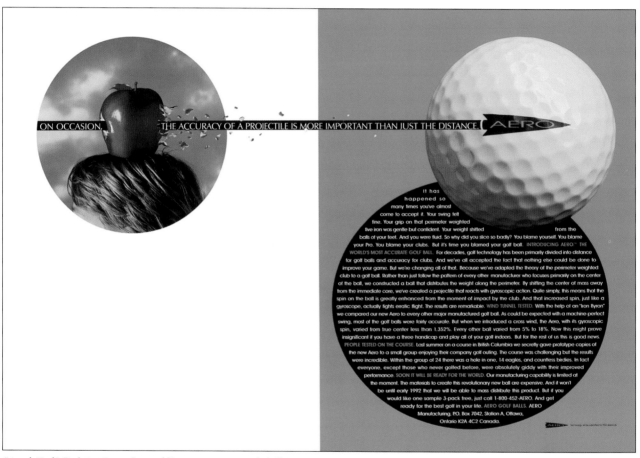

"April Fool's" ad for Aero, the world's most accurate golf ball.

"But they have friends on the inside of all the places."

"We'll make it a new car from a new manufacturer."

"One phone call and they'll sniff it out."

"We'll make it a new car from a new manufacturer from a new car country…Argentina."

"Why Argentina?"

"Why not?"

"But how are you going to produce ads if the car doesn't exist?"

"Like I said, we'll create it."

Then came the hard part. Doing it.

This felt a little like Neil Simon boasting to everyone at a posh party that he was thinking of taking a few weeks to write a new comedic play that would leave audiences in New York laughing, crying and applauding. After his confident announcement, all that would be left for Neil to do would be to sit down and simply do it. (Scratch that. Everyone knows Neil Simon. He has related industry experience. This was like Howie Bushwacker writing the play. You never heard of Howie? That's my point.)

But the strength of our agency is the combined talents we bring to any assignment. This would be no different.

Jim McGavick is the smartest man I know. In the eight years I worked with Jim, there was never a technical question that he couldn't answer. He's just like the old Mr. Wizard on TV. Actually, better than Mr. Wizard. Jim's knowledge goes a lot further than putting vinegar and baking soda in a bottle to pop a cork. Jim could plot the course of the trajectory.

I've always wished that a four-wheel drive car would be easier to control off-road. So I asked Jim if it would be possible to create such a car.

"Oh, yeah," he replied confidently, "no problem. See, what you have with most cars is that the steering column is directly attached to the main frame. If you added suspension to the column, like this"— he was already sketching on the back of a note pad — "you'd eliminate a lot of the vibration. But I think I'd want to add an onboard computer that would compensate for some of the bigger jolts. And then I'd blah blah blah blah blah …" It's at about this point in the conversations with Jim when he enters a dimension that most of us reach only with long, slow logic. Jim keeps grabbing you, trying to pull you along.

"Are you following? Huh? You look confused."

"Jim," I said, "just write it all down and I'll sort it out."

"No problem. 'Cuz in a very related way within the heavy construction industry if you look at the extended steering on those big front end loaders and . . ."

In two days I had a complete picture of what it would take to make this car work. I took that information to Frank Quadflieg. Frank was one of our top graphic designers with an extensive background in industrial design. He had studied and worked in Europe. In fact, Frank would even return once a year to teach at the University of Bruges. In less than a week I had a color illustration that was so comprehensive, it was photo-realistic.

Now we needed a name.

This was important. It would help set the personality for the car. "How about Caballo?" Reed Allen, the art director, suggested. "It means horse in Spanish. And it's perfect for an all-terrain vehicle."

The more we talked about it, the better it sounded.

With Jim's input I wrote the copy over a long weekend.

Reed created the layouts and even added some unique touches, like bordering the headlines in rocks.

Frank created a logo that fit the name. The ads were near completion. Now, what the heck would we do with them?

Another flash of insight. We'd send them directly to the marketing executives at

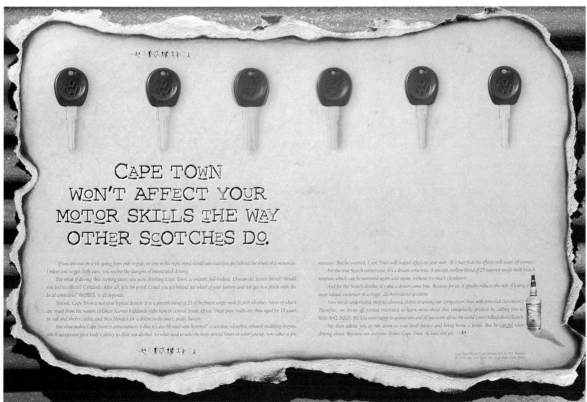

"April Fool's" ads for Cape Town, the only Scotch with Retrohol to sober you within hours of drinking.

the various auto companies. But not from us. Instead, they would come from a British representative of a worldwide market research company. He would be using the reprints to prove that his market research company had unique insight into foreign markets. His company had "discovered" these ads that were soon scheduled for publication in Australia and New Zealand (we made all measurements metric) but could serve as competition in the near future. A representative, Tom Jordan, would contact them sometime soon requesting a capability presentation.

And what better way to fool them than to send it ...oh, say, at the very end of March and reveal on April Fool's Day that it was a prank. April Fool's is the only official day people will forgive you if you trick them.

In essence, we were one of the pioneers in the "April Fool's venue" which others quickly adopted.

The list was assembled, the reprints were collated, and we did some last-minute checking to make sure we could pull it off. We decided to send each person on our list one reprint a day. The first day we would include the cover letter that explained the business of Hoffman York PLC, London. The second and third day we would send only the reprints.

Everything was sent Federal Express. Now here's something we discovered that is rather unique: Federal Express lets you fill in any return address you want. So even though everything was sent from Milwaukee, we could make it appear that it was sent from anywhere.

This way, we were able to make Thomas Jordan, the gadabout representative of Hoffman York PLC, send these reprints as he (supposedly) traveled across America.

Day One, the ads were "sent from" the Plaza Hotel in New York. Day Two, they were "sent from" The Ritz in Chicago. And Day Three, they arrived from The Fairmont in San Francisco. Reservations were made in my name at each hotel . . . just in case someone should call.

On March 27, the day the first mailing arrived at our 63 different auto execs, I

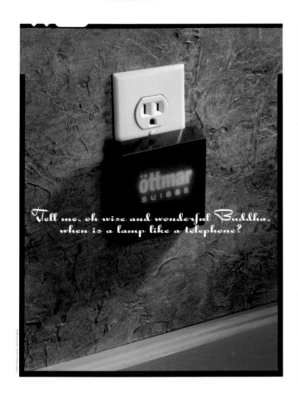

Tell me, oh wise and wonderful Buddha, when is a lamp like a telephone?

Big hint: Telephones can be cordless, therefore portable.

Introducing Total Home Remote Electricity. From one single source, electricity can now be safely projected throughout your entire home. Lamps no longer will need cords. Mixers can operate anywhere. Your stereo can be in the middle of the den.

How is it possible? It started with a dream. Many years ago, a man named Nikola Tesla believed that someday we'd be able to safely project electrons from a single source to power a variety of electrical products. And he came close to succeeding. But after his death in 1943, it took years to put the puzzle together.

What he overlooked, our engineers found. By taking the traditional three wires (one grounded, the other two rated at 110 volts at 60 cycles each) and feeding a central power distribution unit, we've added a

patented projector which emits a safe electrical "aura." Each electrical appliance is secured with a small solid-state converter which is sensitive to the emitted aura. In turn, full current electric power becomes available everywhere.

Your Total Home Remote Electricity unit simply plugs into any outlet in the house. Each and every electrical product can be easily modified to work with Total Home Remote Electricity. One unit safely projects an electrical aura that covers three full floors in an average home. (Our free brochure explains the complete technology and how easy and economical it is to convert each of your present electrical objects.)

Call 1-800-243-3090. It's wise. It's wonderful. It's time.

TOTAL HOME
REMOTE ELECTRICITY

In your wildest dreams, did you ever imagine making toast on your roof?

Fortunately, we did.

Introducing Total Home Remote Electricity. From one single source, electricity can now be safely projected throughout your entire home. Lamps no longer need cords. Mixers can operate anywhere. Your stereo can be in the middle of the den. And, with the help of a ladder, you can make toast on the roof of your house.

How is it possible? It started with a dream. Many years ago, a man named Nikola Tesla believed that someday we'd be able to safely project electrons from a single source to power a variety of electrical products. And he came close to succeeding. But after his death in 1943, it took years to put the puzzle together.

What he overlooked, our engineers found. By taking the traditional three wires (one grounded, the other two rated at 110 volts at 60 cycles each) and feeding a central power distribution unit, we've

added a patented projector which emits a safe electrical "aura." Each electrical appliance is secured with a small solid-state converter which is sensitive to the emitted aura. In turn, full current electric power becomes available everywhere.

Your Total Home Remote Electricity unit simply plugs into any outlet in the house. Each and every electrical product can be easily modified to work with Total Home Remote Electricity. One unit safely projects an electrical aura that covers three full floors in an average home. (Our free brochure explains the complete technology and how easy and economical it is to convert each of your present electrical objects.)

Call 1-800-243-3090. Sometimes, even your wildest dreams come true.

TOTAL HOME
REMOTE ELECTRICITY

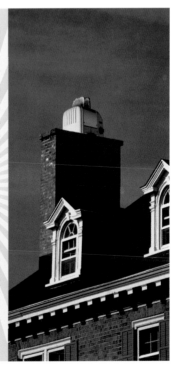

These pre-tour ads for Remote Electricity generated an avalanche of phone calls.

waited until late afternoon to call the Plaza Hotel.

"Hi," I began, "I had an unconfirmed reservation that I unfortunately couldn't keep. Could you tell me if there were any messages for Thomas Jordan?"

"Well Mr. Jordan," the dry, somewhat haughty voice began, "it is not our policy to take phone messages for guests who do not arrive. However, I must admit there were quite a few phone calls for you."

Eureka! They were buying it. They were trying to find out what was going on.

Patiently we waited for the completion of the mailing. We sent letters to arrive via Federal Express explaining the prank as a way of demonstrating our ad agency's capabilities.

I followed up with phone calls to most of the key people on the list. They all admitted that they fell for it hook, line and sinker. In fact, some of the marketing execs sent the ads on to engineering wanting to know if, and when, their company would match this technology.

The Wall Street Journal picked up on it and featured it two days later.

At the end of most new business presentations we conclude by saying, "Maybe we don't have direct industry experience with your business. But again, we don't have any car experience either. Let's show you some car advertising we created. We think it proves a point."

The following year we extended our April Fool's scam to create "Aero," the world's most accurate golf ball. Same scenario, same results.

(And currently Spalding has a line of golf balls called Aero…same name…same typeface. And they were on our mailing list…what a coincidence.)

We followed that with "Capetown," the world's first Scotch with Retrohol, an ingredient that countered the effects of alcohol. It would sober you up within hours of drinking. For this we included an 800 number. The calls from Kentucky were most inspiring. (But in the interest of confidentiality, I can't tell you what they said.)

Our latest April Fool's product innovation was modular electricity. This generated a ton of calls including the president of a vacuum cleaner manufacturing company who insisted, "I must have this."

What does all this prove?

Capability. Insight. Uniqueness. A point of difference.

As a smaller agency struggling to keep your head above water, you have to find unique ways to open eyes, be considered and stand out as a creative force.

For us it was creating cars and golf balls. Who knows what you will discover? ❧

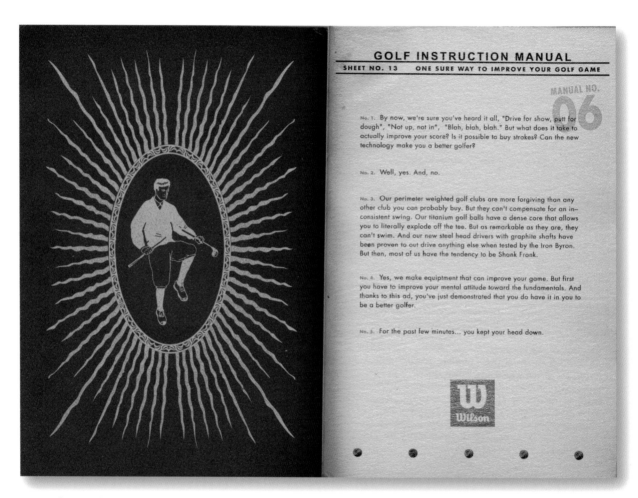

GOLF INSTRUCTION MANUAL

SHEET NO. 13   ONE SURE WAY TO IMPROVE YOUR GOLF GAME

MANUAL NO.
06

No. 1. By now, we're sure you've heard it all, "Drive for show, putt for dough", "Not up, not in", "Blah, blah, blah." But what does it take to actually improve your score? Is it possible to buy strokes? Can the new technology make you a better golfer?

No. 2. Well, yes. And, no.

No. 3. Our perimeter weighted golf clubs are more forgiving than any other club you can probably buy. But they can't compensate for an in-consistent swing. Our titanium golf balls have a dense core that allows you to literally explode off the tee. But as remarkable as they are, they can't swim. And our new steel head drivers with graphite shafts have been proven to out drive anything else when tested by the Iron Byron. But then, most of us have the tendency to be Shank Frank.

No. 4. Yes, we make equipment that can improve your game. But first you have to improve your mental attitude toward the fundamentals. And thanks to this ad, you've just demonstrated that you do have it in you to be a better golfer.

No. 5. For the past few minutes... you kept your head down.

Spec work that didn't win us business.

Chapter 7

Perhaps the most demanding, frustrating, and yet necessary part of our business is the pursuit of new clients. Agencies our size that don't win new business on a regular basis run the risk of drying up. Because sooner or later, regardless of the work you do, someone is going to fire you.

new business.

it's not just a job, it's an adventure.

It's just a fact of life. New marketing managers come in, a key contact at the client is promoted out of your reach, or one of your account people mouths off at a social event and the first time you learn of it is when you're told you're to "be included" in the review.

Another fact of life is that if your account is put up for review, it is not yours to win. So seldom does an incumbent agency retain a business that when they do, that alone is worthy of trade press headlines. (One of the sure signs: You have lunch with them and they insist on picking up the check. Quit now.)

The mistake a lot of agencies make is that they take everything personally. This isn't a college fraternity. It's more like the Mafia. When Sonny Corleone was riddled with bullets, it wasn't personal. It was business.

Every day at our agency we remind each other that we have to focus on our primary missions. First and foremost, our mission is to keep the business we have. Second is to grow the business we have. Third is to get new business.

Missions one and two usually account for about 45 hours or more of the week. But knowing that sooner or later one of your accounts is going to hear the Sirens call from another shop, you have to actively work at getting included in new business activity.

Now if you're Fallon McElligott or Wieden+Kennedy, new business might be a drag, but their reputations (well deserved) open a lot of doors. For the rest of us, we could quote Satchel Paige: "The aheader I go, the behinder I get."

They say that the first casualty of war is the truth. The first casualty of new business is the ego. (Like I said, we tend to take it personally.) I've seen people who could present fast on their feet, out-talk a New York cabbie, trade barbs with stand-up comics and write strategic plans that deserve to be in the Harvard Business Review actually panic when it comes to picking up the phone and making a cold call.

To begin with, the secretary answers the phone. His or her job is to prevent people like you from disrupting the boss. And, to the secretary, you're as annoying as an insurance salesman. Even worse, the secretary has never heard of you or your agency, and will go to great lengths to let you know it.

They will ask if you'd care to leave your number. Don't. When was the last time you called back an insurance agent? Same thing.

Spec work that didn't win us business.

Some people actually think they are making progress by leaving their number. It's a real convenient out. "No, I haven't connected yet with Bill Gates. But I've got a call into him." Let's see, he'll return the President's call later this afternoon, ring up Donald Trump for a little golf and, oh yeah, track down that account guy in Milwaukee who tried to reach him.

The secret to new business is simple: Be incredibly good, extremely personable and professional, be the exact size the client needs, in a location they prefer, with an account team in place, and oh yeah, make sure they know all of this before they look for an agency.

The secret to winning a spot on the Olympic 400-meter relay team is just as simple. Run the hundred in nine flat.

New business is hard work. There are seldom home runs. It's a lot of bunts and singles and pop flies, sacrifice flies and close calls. And today, more than ever, it is competitive.

The quickest way to find out what other agencies do is to ask your own clients. Lloyd Hickson, the ad manager at Oster used to show me all the clever mailings he'd receive. Individually, they were pretty good. Collectively, there was a sameness to them that made you numb.

And once the word reaches the street that an account is up for grabs, the odds of being included reduce dramatically. Years ago we were fortunate to be included in the review for a national pet food. After the presentation I asked the ad manager if he'd heard from a lot of other agencies.

His eyes widened. "Follow me," he said, leading me around a corner to an empty office. There, from floor to ceiling, were portfolios, tapes and boxes from agencies all over the country.

"Was there anything here that impressed you?" I asked.

"Who could possibly have time to be impressed?"

Well, I was impressed. Also depressed. We had tried the same tactics before. When the Reebok Shoe account was up for review, we nuked a pair of Air Jordans

Spec work that didn't win us business.

"I USE ECHO® HEDGE CLIPPERS BECAUSE THEY'RE AS OBSESSIVE AS I AM." *Hank Stram, Green Acres Landscaping*

CUTS THROUGH TREE TRUNKS, LOGS, BRUSH
AND THE OCCASIONAL AUDI.

IT DOESN'T EAT WEEDS. IT DECAPITATES THEM.

Spec work that didn't win us business.

and put them in an ammo box with a message: "Some agencies will promise to capture greater market share." (Open the box to reveal the torched shoes.) "We take no prisoners."

We learned later someone cut their finger trying to open the box. No . . . they didn't call us.

When we were in a final competition for a piece of business, competing head-to-head with the client's current agency who had a well publicized on-again off-again romance with each other, we sent a picture of Elizabeth Taylor and included a little history.

"In 1962 Liz said she loved Richard Burton and would never leave him. In 1967 she filed for divorce. After publicly trading barbs in the press, Liz and Richard were reunited in 1972. Liz said she loved Richard and would never leave him. In 1975 Liz again filed for divorce. Richard despaired and died a poor pathetic creature.

In 1990 your agency said they loved you and would never leave you . . ."

For some reason that one struck a chord and we were invited to the pitch.

You have to be tenacious in your quest to get in and apply the same creative thinking you would to create advertising. Troy Peterson, our business director, loves leaving voice mail. Most others are put off by it, mutter something and then hang up. Troy prepares exactly what he wants to say and takes advantage of this one-sided debate. And no one can hang up. So he politely points out the reasons to include us and doesn't have to worry about someone cutting him off. A good percentage of the time, they return his call.

We found the best reception to mailed capabilities pieces occurs when some-one talks with (or preferably meets) the prospect before any material arrives on their desk.

* * *

If your new business operation is going to succeed it has to be top-of-mind for the entire agency. You'll be asking people to drop everything on a weekend and pitch in. They have to know why and buy into the need to sacrifice for the effort.

In order to get cooperation from everyone here we tried a variety of methods.

But one really worked. We created an incentive that would rally the entire agency: a three-day cruise in the Caribbean if we met a certain goal.

We decided that if we got *$10* million in new billing . . . and didn't lose any billing at the same time . . . why not?

The entire agency was assembled. The plan was laid out. Hoots and hollers from every corner. This looked like a win/win. If we got $10 million (highly unlikely) the agency goes on a cruise. If we got somewhat less (highly likely) we come out ahead and don't have to pay for anything.

But something strange happened. People really started pulling together like never before. Magazine reps that heard about it thought it was really unique and started feeding us leads on any piece of business they thought was loose. People were staying even later to finish work to allow time for new business development. An incredibly strong "gung ho" attitude was everywhere.

And it was paying off.

By March we had $4 million in new business. By July we had nearly $6 million. The end of summer was one frustration after another. A little here, a little there. It was late in the fall, when we were starting to despair, that we won the entire Outboard Marine business: Johnson Outboards, Evinrude, and all the parts and accessories. That put us at $12 million in new business.

And to really make it official, Mike Wanniger, who was the Marketing Manager at OMC, agreed to announce the win to the agency. A solid shout of joy over a new business win was the first reaction. But slowly the reality set in over the agency: This meant we were really going on *the cruise.*

Pandemonium broke. There was dancing on the conference room tables. A "pre-cruise" party was immediately arranged. We hired a reggae band and set up tropical drinks and food outside our building. When we would explain the reason for the party to people passing by, they all had the same reply: "Gee, I wish I worked at a place like that."

Something else happened. Nobody quit.

There's usually some turnover right after the first of the year. But no one wanted to miss out on the three-day cruise in the Caribbean.

We were scheduled to leave Milwaukee at 9:00 a.m. on Friday, February 4th. At 5:00 that morning I received a frantic call from the travel agent.

"There's an unbelievable snow storm that's going to get even worse. They're telling me they're going to close down the airport. But there's a 7:30 a.m. flight. If you can get the whole agency on it, you might be okay."

"Alright," I replied, more than a little skeptically, "who the hell is this? Who is this really?"

The woman started to get a little upset. "Just look out your window."

The world was covered with snow and it was falling hard. A big Buick was fish-tailing down the street. It was wet, heavy snow. The trees were all leaning. I could end up spending all morning cleaning up the sidewalks. Or, if I hustled, I could be in the Caribbean.

"Okay," I said, "I'll handle it." And I sprang into action. I did what all good agency executives in times of crisis do. I called an account person.

But not just any account person. I called Joanne Besasie, the most organized person we had. She set up mini-group callers making each responsible for getting five or six people contacted. Then she cross-referenced others as a follow-up.

By 7:00 a.m., despite the fact that all of Milwaukee was practically closed and the streets were deserted, the entire agency was at the airport.

But it was too soon to celebrate. They had already closed the airport.

Buses were hired. A flight from Chicago was arranged. We were racing the clock . . . and the storm. We made it to O'Hare and we were the last flight to lift off before they closed the airport.

Several hours later as the boat pulled away from the dock in Ft. Lauderdale, a self-satisfied feeling covered the entire group. We were off to three days of non-stop partying while the rest of our friends were shoveling out driveways and trying to stay warm.

It was that commitment that got us into quite a few pitches.

* * *

As hard as it is to get up to bat, the hardest, most crucial part is to maximize the opportunity once you get there. Again, you might be tempted to swing for the fences and show them complete campaigns. But this is a subjective business. And it's a little premature to think that you can solve their problems without their input. It's so easy for anyone on their side to say "no" when you show creative work. And any "no" could bounce you out. So prove you're smart, insightful and fun to be with but try to avoid speculative creative at all costs.

For starters, have you discovered what problems your prospective clients believe they face? This may sound basic, but it's often overlooked. Their most compelling issue might be dealer recruitment, expensive locations, a poor reputation for service or inconsistent product quality. Ask them. Seldom does a prospect say, "We're looking for really edgy ads that no one can read."

And see if you can get a hold of the research they've already done.

They've paid for it. And chances are they believe in it.

Make sure you look for the questions that weren't asked and find a way to fill those holes. It's been said that clients are the most receptive when you tell them 75 percent of what they already know and 25 percent of what they don't know.

Any case history you show them has to somehow relate to helping them solve their problems. If not, why are you showing it to them?

Please don't bore them. Find a refreshing way to present your insight that will help them remember you and like you for not showing light bulbs and ships about to collide or question marks . . . you know, PowerPoint 101?

We like to take all the information we've gathered and enlarge it and pin it to the wall. This allows everyone to immerse themselves in the project. And when the data you gathered is shared with your prospect in this manner, it allows them to stare at the unique nuggets you uncovered. They often get up and move around the room. It allows them to ask questions. They become more involved. And that's key to winning.

And after you win a pitch, be humble. If you're not, you'll become humble soon enough. All you have to do is pick up the phone, call the next prospect, reach the secretary and relive the litany:

"Now, who are you? Is that an advertising agency? How do you spell that? Would you care to leave your number?" ✪

Chapter 8

Undoubtedly, you have a stable of talent ready to

prove to the world that they are capable of break-

through thinking and creative insight that will make

the entire advertising industry look in your direction

put your ambitions to good use.

public service advertising.

and offer unsolicited praise. Trouble is, when most of

the assignments you have are, say, working for a

bank that insists you include the interest rate, a

picture of their president and 25 lines of qualifying

copy, there isn't a lot of opportunity to showcase

your potential.

That can be frustrating because clients will only buy the advertising that they believe to be the best for them. Sometimes we make the mistake of feeling like we're doctors and that our clients should just do what we tell them. We're not doctors. We're more like architects. Some of your clients will sometimes insist on something that doesn't make sense to you…like making the logo bigger… or putting an exclamation mark at the end of the headline. That would be the equivalent of telling an architect that you want a skylight with a western exposure. They'd tell you that southern light is the best. That you *have* to have southern exposure. But you don't care, it's your money. If they can't convince you in terms that are compelling to you, you will have it your way. If they kick up a fuss and make you feel stupid, you just might fire them.

It's up to us to propose, but it's your client's right to dispose. That doesn't mean we shouldn't be well prepared to sell them the merits of innovative thinking, but some just might insist on something that makes them more comfortable. Now some purists would say, "Fire them," and a lot of agencies have done that. Unfortunately, many of those agencies are now out of business. Clients that are willing to let you swing for the fences are so rare that agencies fight each other for them. It was once said that great clients make great agencies. That's still true. That's why Nike, Budweiser, ESPN and a few others do award-winning work…regardless of the agency they work with.

The premise for this book is survival. To us, that means being somewhat schizophrenic. As I tell the creative people all the time, "I owe you a One Show opportunity every once in a while, but I owe you a paycheck every day." This isn't quite the cop-out it appears to be. If you're patient and smart, you can gradually open the minds of your safe, conservative clients by slowly bringing them in to innovative approaches. What works best is when you can take them out of the equation. Show them what clients in other categories did to break out of the pack and explain how successful it was. Do this when there is nothing for sale. Plant seeds. Embracing a different point of view can be frightening for some. It takes time.

So, what are you supposed to do in the meantime? You have all this creative energy, all this ambition and few chances to shine.

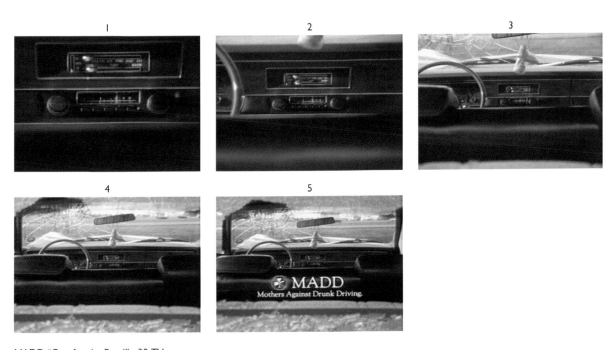

MADD "One for the Road" :30 TV

1-5 Song: One for my baby, one for the
   road.
   Visual: Opens on close-up of a car
   radio. Pulls out throughout song to
   reveal baby shoes on rearview mirror
   and cracked window from accident.

5 Logo: MADD

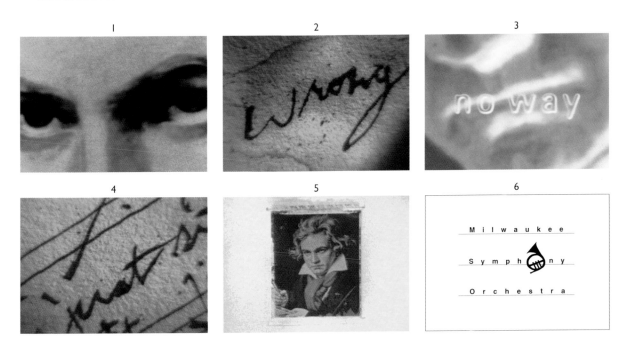

Symphony "Beethoven" :30 TV

1 Female VO: I don't know what's wrong
   with him. He's just so different. That hair,
   the way he dresses…

2 And get a real job? No way.

3 He just sits in his room and plays music
   I've never heard before.

4 I tell him he'll never make anything of
   himself, but he just won't listen.

5 Announcer: He dedicated his entire life
   to music. Why not dedicate a few
   beautiful moments?

6 LOGO: Milwaukee Symphony Orchestra

Exotic Male Dancers Performing Nightly

INDIAN SUMMER 1988
MILWAUKEE LAKEFRONT • SEPTEMBER 9, 10, 11

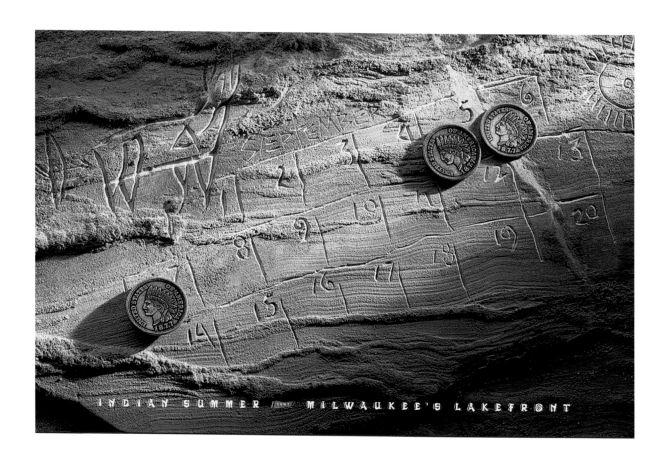

INDIAN SUMMER / 1997 MILWAUKEE'S LAKEFRONT

INDIAN SUMMER 1991. MILWAUKEE LAKEFRONT. SEPTEMBER 6,7,8.

IF YOU REALLY WANT TO BE SOMEBODY, PRACTICE USING THE ONE ON THE RIGHT.

USE YOUR HEAD. LEARN.

P.O. BOX 10754 MINNEAPOLIS, MN 55458-3754 612-933-6745

PAGE
EDUCATION FOUNDATION

1

2

3

4

5

DON'T BE A PINHEAD.

USE YOUR HEAD. LEARN.

Page Foundation "Pinhead" :30 TV

1 Boy talking in alley: Okay, this is how it is. School? There ain't nothin' in a book that I can't find out and learn for myself.

2 The teachers are trying to tell me, "If you don't use it, you lose it. You've got to exercise your mind."

3 Me? I'm thinking, you're so smart, why you still in school?

4 And I don't need no schools or no teachers to tell me how to do it. That's how it is. So understand that.

5 Got it? Good.

DON'T BE A PINHEAD.

USE YOUR HEAD. LEARN.

P.O. BOX 10754 MINNEAPOLIS, MN 55458-3754 612-933-6745

PAGE
EDUCATION FOUNDATION

If Your Child Suddenly Comes To Mind, Call Us.

PARENTS ANONYMOUS 291-7285

Blood Center "Listen" :30 TV

1-3 Visual: Man speaking to camera, but no sound.

4 VO: No matter how hard we try to deliver this message, some people don't listen.

5 Title Card: You can't get aids from donating blood.

6 Logo: The Blood Center

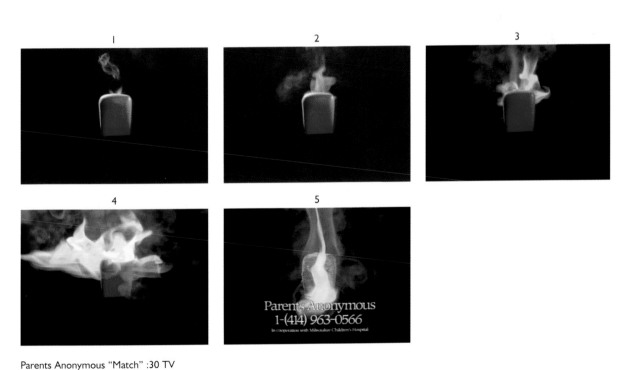

Parents Anonymous "Match" :30 TV

1 Man: Will that baby ever stop crying?

2 Woman: How long does it take to toilet train this kid?

3 VO: It's natural for parents to become angry...

4 Woman: I'm sick and tired of dressing you every single day.

5 But when you're temper is ready to flare out of control, you may need a friend.
Logo: Parents Anonymous

Need to Read "Titles" :30 TV

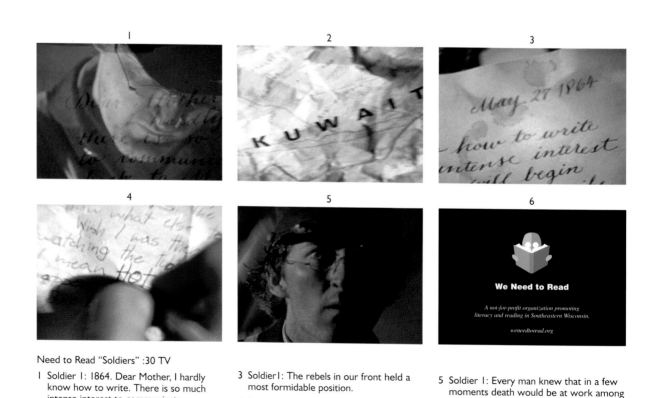

Need to Read "Soldiers" :30 TV

1 Soldier 1: 1864. Dear Mother, I hardly know how to write. There is so much intense interest to communicate.

2 Soldier 2: 1991. Hi guys, got your package — been munching on chips ... I wish we could just get this over with — morale sucks.

3 Soldier1: The rebels in our front held a most formidable position.

4 Soldier 2: Wish I was there kicking back, watching the tube. It's hot as hell here and I mean hot!

5 Soldier 1: Every man knew that in a few moments death would be at work among us.

6 Logo card.
Soldier 2: I just want something to happen. Drop me a line. Later gator.

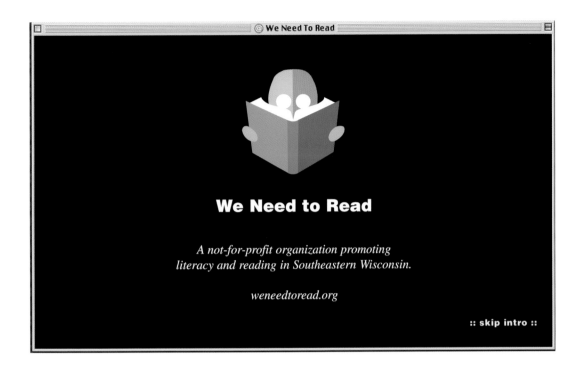

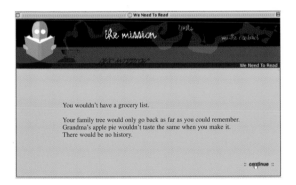

Turning a website into a portal to fight illiteracy and to instill in people a desire to read.

Well, believe it or not, you are surrounded by opportunities. There are organizations all around you that would love your help, love your insight, reward your efforts and embrace your creative thinking. There are dozens of non-profit organizations that will allow you to show the world how good you really are. (Good here has multiple meanings.)

The big agencies go after the big organizations. They have all the bureaucracy of real clients ... tons of committees ... multiple approvals, etc. You have the chance to get in with local organizations. And that's better. For starters, most aren't sophisticated marketers. That's good ... bad ... and good. Good because they will often look to you for answers. Bad because you will discover that despite your ambitions you have a conscience that won't let you create irresponsible advertising because these well-intentioned people actually trust you. Good because more than likely the result of that conscience and your talent will result in effective marketing that will actually make a difference.

Another advantage of taking on pro-bono work is that suppliers will often jump on board to help if they believe in the cause as well. We've had printers, photographers, editors and directors all donate their time and often their out-of-pocket expenses to help produce public service advertising. And, if it truly is distinctive and breakthrough, media will cooperate as well. Television stations are required by law to air a certain amount of public service advertising. The cheap, convoluted, video productions that were done in-house by an organization will appear at 4:00 a.m., after the infomercial for self-administered cosmetic surgery. We've seen the PSAs we've produced on the evening news and prime time television. The station managers want to get credit as well for showing something that's really good.

Remnants of magazine space that isn't sold often goes to PSAs. And they too would rather showcase something provocative and effective than a busy ad with a grainy photo and tons of copy.

This is also a chance to get the entire agency involved with a good cause. It's another opportunity to pull together and work as a team.

The other by-product of these efforts is that you feel pretty good about yourself when the organization tells you they received more phone calls in one week than they got all year ... thanks to your advertising.

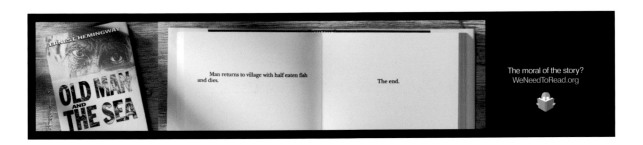

Man returns to village with half eaten fish and dies.

The end.

The moral of the story?
WeNeedToRead.org

Boys stranded on desert island kill each other.

The end.

The moral of the story?
WeNeedToRead.org

1

2

CAPITOL BREWING CO.
1933 – 1948

3

4

BLATZ BREWING CO.
1846 – 1959

5

SAVE THE
MILWAUKEE BREWERS

6

SUPPORT
MILLER PARK

SPONSORED BY HOFFMAN YORK & COMPTON

Miller Park :30 TV

1-5 SFX: Crowd cheering.

6 VO: How many brewers does Milwaukee have to lose before we finally wake up?

1

2

3

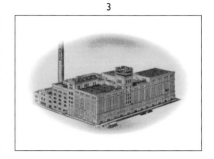

4

5

SPORTS
Morrison Announces
He's HIV Positive

6

AIDS hits
Heterosexuals too.

Tommy Morrison :30 TV

1 Visual: Animated shots of Tommy Morrison.
Audio: Song, "The Wanderer."

5 Visual: Headline from newspaper: "Tommy Morrison Announces He's HIV Positive."
Audio: Song skips on lyric, "Going nowhere."

6 Logo: AMFAR

In new business presentations a generous sprinkling of great PSAs show the prospect two things: 1) this is an agency that is willing to give back to the community, and 2) the thinking and execution are incredible. (Not a bad net take-away if you're trying to win a piece of business.)

Recently, we took this initiative one step further. We decided to champion a cause that the entire agency believes in. Reading. We created our own organization, "We Need To Read," a non-profit organization promoting literacy and reading in Southeastern Wisconsin. We have our own website (weneedtoread.org) that serves as a portal to literacy services, libraries, tutors and book stores that promote literacy and reading. All of our PSAs for this organization direct people to this website for further information. In addition to advertising, our staff is encouraged to volunteer as reading tutors, read to classrooms, distribute books, and anything else they can think of to promote the written word.

The same opportunities exist for you. Look around, find a good cause or two. Get involved. Use your talents. Make a difference. And feel good about it. ❧

1

2

3

4

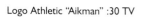

5

6

Logo Athletic "Aikman" :30 TV

1 Troy Aikman: There's some tough birds in our division who love putting the ache in Aikman.

2 And those people in Washington, definitely believe in capital punishment.

3 Even when things are good, I remember, there are stills Giant in New York.

4 Do I think winning another Super Bowl is going to be easy?

5 GET REAL.

6 VO: Logo Athletic, authentic team apparel.

Chapter 9

I never advocate technique for the sake of technique.

But if technology provides techniques that allow you

to realize an idea, make sure you fully investigate the

opportunities it might offer.

don't just embrace technology.

Give it a bear hug.

A few years ago we developed a campaign for Logo

Athletic, a sports apparel company headquartered in

Indianapolis. They had signed some of the top pro-

fessional athletes to endorse their line of clothing.

The problem was, so had every other sports clothes

company.

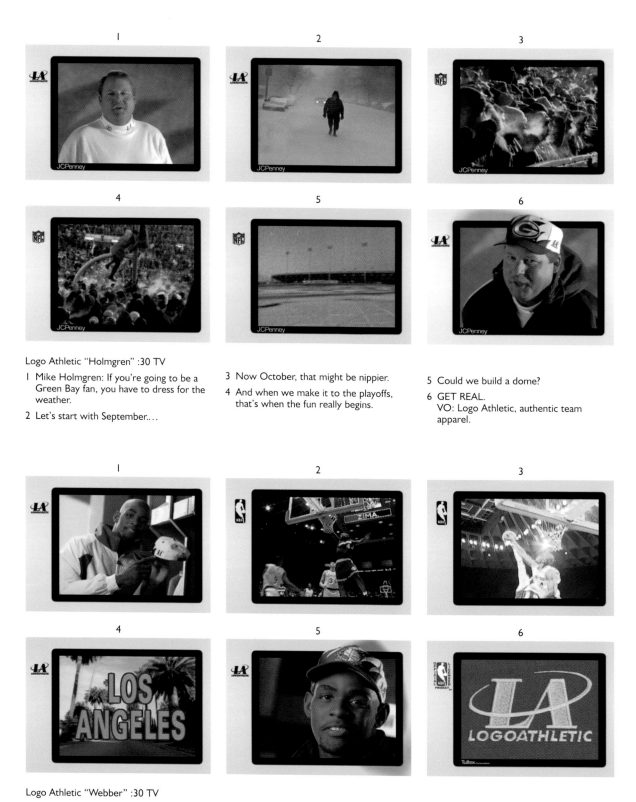

Logo Athletic "Holmgren" :30 TV

1 Mike Holmgren: If you're going to be a Green Bay fan, you have to dress for the weather.

2 Let's start with September....

3 Now October, that might be nippier.

4 And when we make it to the playoffs, that's when the fun really begins.

5 Could we build a dome?

6 GET REAL.
  VO: Logo Athletic, authentic team apparel.

Logo Athletic "Webber" :30 TV

1 Chris Webber: You know, a lot of people ask me what the LA stands for.

2 Low altitude? Don't think so.

3 Laid-back attitude? No way.

4 Los Angeles?

5 GET REAL.

6 VO: Logo Athletic, official NBA licensed apparel.

To emphasize the authentic, genuine clothing Logo had for sale, we developed a battle cry: "Get Real." For TV we wanted to drive the point home by creating engaging dialogue with each athlete, interspersed with action shots that emphasized the irony of their comments.

But we wanted more. We wanted to own the TV screen and have a visual signature that made us stand apart from the competition. Mike Wheaton, who was the art director, had been studying the ability of a relatively new editing technique called "The Flame" and created a fast, cost-effective way to split the images and give the spot an almost 3-D effect. This was not just a gimmick; it gave the message more meaning, life and a distinctive property.

The results were amazing. Not only did it help overcome the somewhat stiff deliveries of some of the athletes, it provided a "wow" factor that made a lasting impression.

The TV advertising was one of the crucial factors that helped propel Logo to second only to Starter in sports apparel … at a fraction of the budget of all other competitors.

Because we stayed current with technology, we were better able to incorporate the latest thinking and not be limited by not knowing what we could or couldn't do.

* * *

Today, more than ever, the small agency can have an added advantage with new technology, new services, new thinking. The Internet has leveled the field like never before. You now have the ability to gather and share information as fast as anyone. And some of the bigger shops are still pushing primarily for network television.

A lot of the bigger shops will talk about "fully integrated marketing solutions" but they don't want to do the tough stuff: the collateral, the website, the outbound telemarketing. They send that to "special departments" inside or outside the agency where the turnover is so high it's hard to keep the names straight.

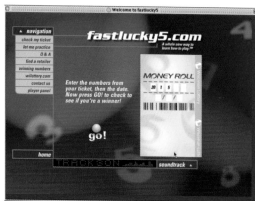

Using the web as a tool to teach consumers how to play a complex new Lottery game.

Utilizing interactivity to its fullest by empowering consumers to learn and apply the principles of "Organomics" online.

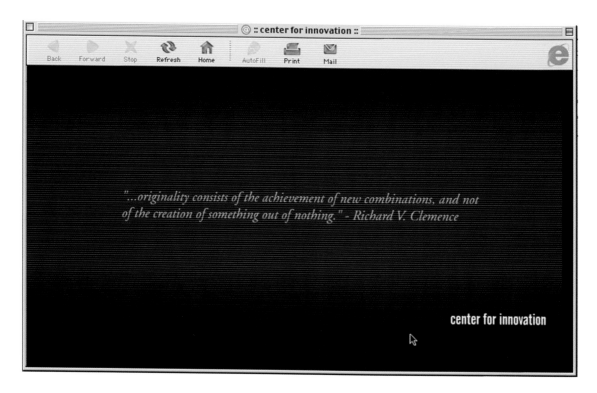

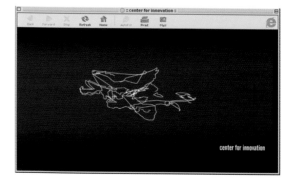

The Center for Innovation website brings the concept of innovation to life in an innovative manner.

The Internet gives you the ability to think of things not previously thought possible, and more importantly, to chart and claim territory in the name of brand building, not just information dissemination.

In communications and mass media, the art of taking a message and delivering it to the masses is still very important. But how many times have you thought, "If we could only bottle the experience of the brand and let everyone share that experience, we'd have converts?" That's the reality of using the Internet as the hub for integrated marketing.

And the beauty is, you don't have to be really big to do it.

But you have to have the right people. And the right mindset.

We work in teams. The teams have to recognize that the rules have changed. Mass media advertising doesn't drive the bus. (It has a front row seat but the "brand building idea" steers us.) We try to operate like the Borg from "Star Trek," a cooperative mindset. The product (ideas) is what we put on a pedestal.

We try to treat the world of the web much the same as other communication tools. We recognize its unique capabilities, but we don't want to be mesmerized by the simple sizzle it can offer. A lot of the bigger providers seem to have a top-down mentality toward web communication . . . what's going to "wow" the client. We want to create functional tools that the sales rep can appreciate. In essence, we're replacing them with a one-on-one dialogue with their customer. (They don't call it "Interactive" for nothing.)

We try not to be snobs about it. Too many providers are using the veil of secrecy of the web to bamboozle clients into believing anything they say, at any price they demand. There will be a day of reckoning when clients become every bit as educated as the web providers and they will realize who was or wasn't straight with them.

The overall message here is to keep your eyes and ears open to whatever the new technology or new buzz might be. There's nothing more awkward than having a client ask you about something new and innovative . . . and you've never even heard of it. ❧

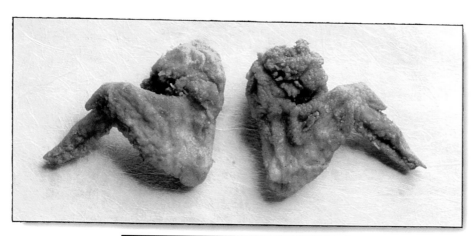

We Have To Earn Our Wings Every Day.

Nobody's Cookin' Like Today's KFC.

Chapter 10

Okay, I'm just about through preaching. I hope there were a few gems that will help you in your quest. Several added suggestions: just like our KFC poster points out, you have to earn your wings every day. You can't slow down. You have to be driven. But one

where do you go from here?

thing you need to do as well is celebrate your success. Every once in awhile, if you win a new piece of business, you get an ad or two in an annual, or you sell that edgy campaign that you knew was right for the client ... bask.

Sit back, relax, congratulate yourselves and enjoy the moment. Tell your fellow employees how good they are, how proud you are. The successes for agencies our size don't happen that often. Make sure you enjoy them. It makes all the hard work worthwhile.

* * *

When I accepted the job at Hoffman York I thought it would provide a great stepping stone to bigger and better opportunities. It would be a chance for me to make a mark. I thought I'd stay three, maybe four, years.

That was 18 years ago.

Milwaukee slowly takes you over. It's peaceful without being boring. Small without being small-minded. Proud without being fanatical. And despite the cold winters, it has the warmest people I've ever met.

This is the hometown you've always read about.

Someone once pointed out to me that our shop has had nine different name changes since the original agency began in Milwaukee in 1933. That reminds me of a joke I read in an *Archie* comic book many years ago. Archie was telling Jughead that he had a hatchet that could be traced all the way back to Alexander the Great. Jughead thought the hatchet looked pretty good for a tool that was that old. Archie explained that the reason it looked so good was that over the years the handle and head had each been replaced five times . . . but it was still the original hatchet. (Think of it . . . there was a time when a comic book expected a kid to know history and understand the humor of irony.)

But where do we go?

The Spanish philosopher Santayana said that those who cannot remember the past are condemned to repeat it. Another famous philosopher, Tom Papanek, my boss at Burnett, approached it from the other end. His motto was "Don't overthink it."

I guess we're somewhere in the middle. We're just renting space. We bought our tickets and we're taking our ride. Every day is a fight to survive.

Good luck to all those like us who fight the same fight. ❧

A special 65 year reunion of Hoffman York

Who is Hoffman York?

We're an independent, full-service communication company headquartered in Milwaukee, Wisconsin. We were the first American advertising agency to buy ourselves back from Saatchi & Saatchi.

In the mid 1980s we were profiled in *Winners* magazine.

In 1998 we were profiled in both *Graphis* and *Print* magazines.

We were one of the first to create the April Fool's ads that others have imitated.

We've been written up in *The Wall Street Journal* and *The New York Times*.

We served as the "Innovation Partner" for Quaker State and created the clear bottle that won the Package of the Year Award.

Our print work is on display at the Museum für Kunst und Gewerbe in Hamburg, Germany.

Our West Coast office was the only western region finalist for the 2000 AAAA O'Toole Awards … after just nine months in business.

Our television commercials have been featured in London, Rome, Tokyo and Stockholm.

We have created and produced over half a dozen original songs that were later used in commercials, including one that was recorded by Ray Charles.

Currently, we bill $80 million and employ 71 people.

We receive resumes from all over the world.

About the author

Tom Jordan is President and Chief Creative Officer of Hoffman York Advertising in Milwaukee, Wisconsin. After creative stints at Leo Burnett and Tatham, Laird & Kudner in Chicago, Tom moved to Wisconsin in 1983 as Creative Director.

His initial goal was to spend a year or two in Milwaukee before moving back to Chicago. But somewhere along the line he, his wife and two sons, all fell in love with Wisconsin.

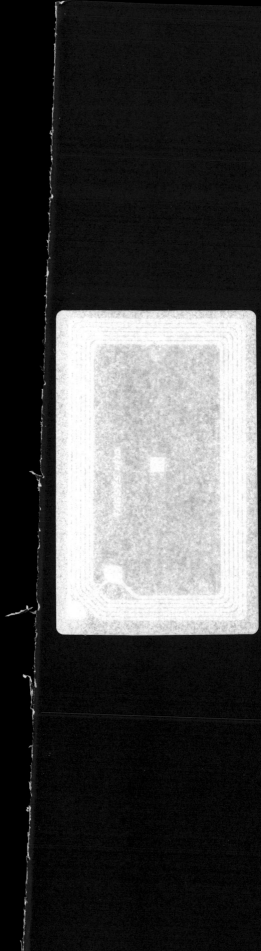